Grammar Practice Book

Scott Foresman

Editorial Offices: Glenview, Illinois • Parsippany, New Jersey • New York, New York
Sales Offices: Reading, Massachusetts • Duluth, Georgia • Glenview, Illinois
Carrollton, Texas • Ontario, California

Editorial Offices
Glenview, Illinois • Parsippany, New Jersey • New York, New York

Sales Offices
Reading, Massachusetts • Duluth, Georgia • Glenview, Illinois
Carrollton, Texas • Ontario, California

ISBN 0-328-00666-1

21 22 23 -DBH-10 09 08

Table of Contents

Unit 2 **Nouns**

Unit 3 Verbs

Unit 4 Adjectives, Adverbs, and Contractions

Unit 5 Pronouns, Prepositions, and Conjunctions

Unit 6 Sentence Parts and Punctuating Sentences

Name ______________________________

Sentences

REVIEW

Directions: Each sentence below is missing a capital letter and an end mark. Write each sentence correctly on the line.

1. my friend Greta was taking a plane trip

____

2. this was Greta's first trip in a plane

____

3. the time for takeoff had arrived

____

4. greta was very excited about her trip

____

5. the plane rushed down the runway and into the air

____

Directions: Use the nouns and verbs to write five sentences on the lines below.

Nouns	Verbs
plane, flight attendant, passenger, clouds, Greta	rushed, soared, announced, talked, floated

6. ______________________________
7. ______________________________
8. ______________________________
9. ______________________________
10. ______________________________

Notes for Home: Your child corrected and wrote sentences. ***Home Activity:*** Have your child write four or five sentences about traveling. Together, check that the word order makes sense and that all sentences are capitalized and punctuated correctly.

Name ____________________

Sentences

A **sentence** is a group of words that tells, asks, commands, or exclaims. It begins with a capital letter and ends with a punctuation mark.

Sentence: I went to a cattle ranch.

Some groups of words are not sentences. You can see whether a group of words is a sentence by checking whether it expresses a complete thought.

Not a Sentence: Cows on a ranch.

Directions: Read the paragraph. Underline the five complete sentences.

1.–5. The cattle were drinking peacefully at the creek. Wolves on a nearby hilltop. The cows lifted their heads and listened. One wolf and another. Crept down the hillside. An old steer bellowed a warning. The frightened herd splashed into the creek. Slipped down the muddy bank and fell. Bawling loudly. The cowhands rode at full speed toward the creek.

Directions: Choose the word group that will complete each sentence. Then write the complete sentence on the line.

6. Every spring the cowhands _____. a cattle drive went on a cattle drive

____

7. _____ huge herds across the plain. Crews of cowhands The cowhands drove

____

8. _____ the wagon carrying their food. Behind them A team of horses pulled

____

9. Each night the cook _____. supper over a campfire made a big pot of beans

____

10. _____ played the fiddle. After dinner Jake After dinner sang and

____

Notes for Home: Your child identified and wrote complete sentences. ***Home Activity:*** Ask your child to describe some activities you have enjoyed together. Have your child use complete sentences. Help your child write some of these sentences.

Name ______________________________

Sentences

Directions: Rewrite each word group so that it is a complete sentence. Add any words you wish to make the sentence. Remember to use capital letters and end punctuation.

1. go to visit Aunt Sue ______________________

2. lives on a fishing boat ______________________

3. sail the boat out to sea ______________________

4. disappears behind us ______________________

5. one day last summer ______________________

6. blew our boat onto a rocky island ______________________

7. huge, hairy gorillas ______________________

8. knew how to speak gorilla language ______________________

9. the gorilla queen ______________________

10. all night under a big full moon ______________________

Write a Speech

On a separate sheet of paper, write a short speech that a gorilla queen could give to welcome strangers to her island. Be sure to use only complete sentences.

Notes for Home: Your child identified and wrote complete sentences. ***Home Activity:*** Encourage your child to think of some things that might happen on a fantasy summer vacation and use complete sentences to express his or her ideas.

Name ____________________________________

RETEACHING

Sentences

The groups of words below are not sentences.

Ray throws the.
Hits the ball.

Write your own words to complete each thought.
Use the picture to help you.

1. Ray throws the________________.

2. ________________ hits the ball.

A **sentence** is a group of words that tells a complete thought. When a group of words does not tell a complete thought, it is not a sentence.

Directions: Circle each group of words that is a sentence.

1. The player is ready to hit the ball.

2. The first strike.

3. She hit a home run.

4. High in the sky and into the crowd.

5. The Aces won the game.

6. On the field with the coach.

7. Swings the bat.

Directions: Write each sentence you circled.

8. ____

9. ____

10. ____

Notes for Home: Your child identified and wrote complete sentences. ***Home Activity:*** Together, write five interesting words on a piece of paper. Have your child use these words in complete sentences to tell a story.

Name ______________________________

Sentences

Directions: Circle the group of words in each pair that is a sentence.

1. Amelia Earhart loved planes.

   Was a famous pilot.

2. First to fly alone from Hawaii to California.

   She broke many flying records.

3. Tried to fly around the world alone.

   Her plane vanished in 1937.

4. Earhart was never found.

   Will always be remembered.

5. Won an award for courage.

   She wrote a book about flying.

Directions: Draw a line to match each group of words on the left to the correct group on the right.

6. People with tickets	carries jet fuel in its tank.
7. A tank truck	check passengers' seat belts.
8. The jet engines	find their seats.
9. The pilot	begin to roar.
10. Flight attendants	carries up to 300 people.
11. The big airplane	knows how to fly the plane.

Write a Paragraph

Write about what you might see from an airplane. Be sure each of your sentences tells a complete thought. Write on a separate sheet of paper.

Notes for Home: Your child identified complete sentences and matched groups of words to create complete sentences. ***Home Activity:*** Have your child use complete sentences to describe a favorite place.

Name ________________________________

Sentences and Sentence Fragments

REVIEW

Directions: Write **S** if the group of words is a sentence. Write **NS** if the group of words is **not** a sentence.

_______________ **1.** Every summer for a week.

_______________ **2.** With my mom, dad, and two sisters.

_______________ **3.** Everyone but my sister Julie can cook.

_______________ **4.** Like to go fishing on the lake.

_______________ **5.** Birdwatching is Dad's favorite activity.

_______________ **6.** A canoe for paddling on the lake.

_______________ **7.** Our kayak can tip too easily for small children to use it.

_______________ **8.** Fortunately, all of us.

_______________ **9.** There is a great cliff for diving.

_______________ **10.** We think camping vacations are the best.

Directions: Circle each group of words above that is **not** a sentence. Rewrite the word group to make it a complete sentence. Add any words you wish to make the sentence.

11. ____

12. ____

13. ____

14. ____

15. ____

Notes for Home: Your child identified sentence fragments and corrected them to make complete sentences. ***Home Activity:*** Help your child read a storybook and identify complete sentences and any word groups that are not complete sentences.

Name ______________________________

Subjects and Predicates

A sentence has a subject and a predicate. The **subject** is the word or group of words about which something is said in the sentence. The **predicate** is the word or group of words that tells something about the subject.

The bears live in the woods.
subject predicate

Directions: Read each sentence. Write **S** if the underlined words are the subject. Write **P** if they are the predicate.

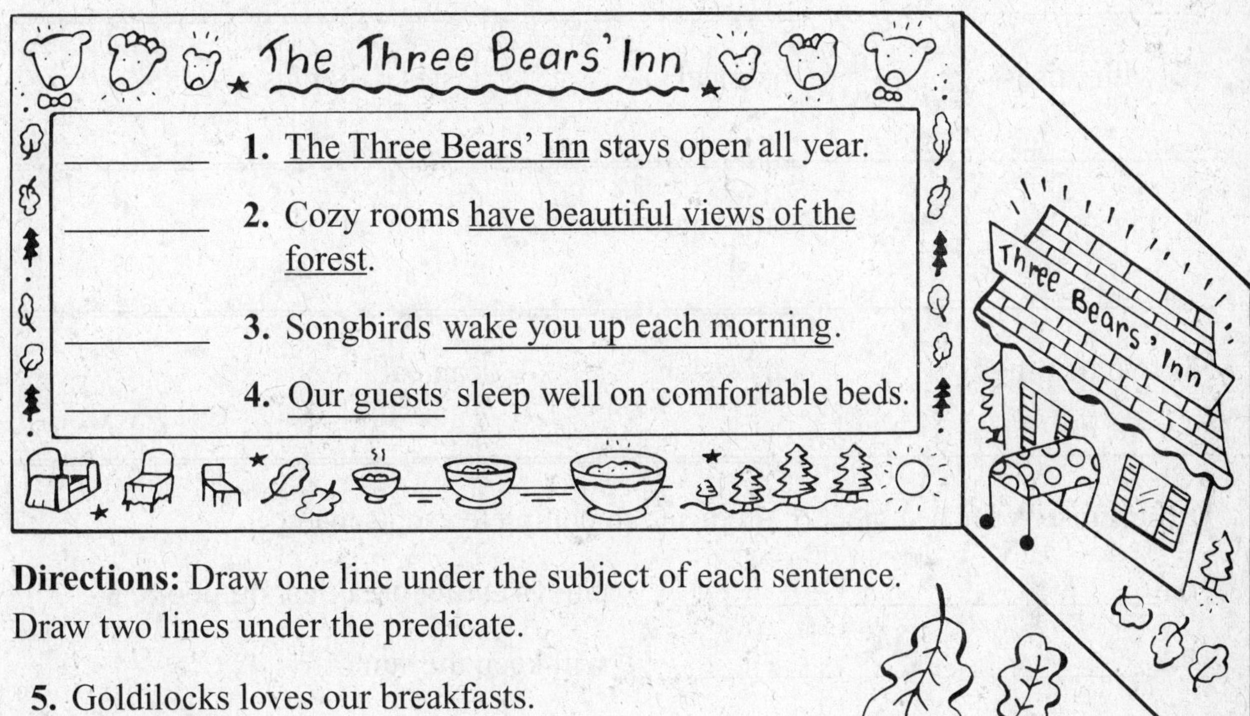

_______ **1.** The Three Bears' Inn stays open all year.

_______ **2.** Cozy rooms have beautiful views of the forest.

_______ **3.** Songbirds wake you up each morning.

_______ **4.** Our guests sleep well on comfortable beds.

Directions: Draw one line under the subject of each sentence. Draw two lines under the predicate.

5. Goldilocks loves our breakfasts.

6. Your children will enjoy our Baby Bear Special.

7. You can find three kinds of porridge on our menu.

8. Papa Bear leads nature walks through the woods.

9. Many families come to enjoy fall in the forest.

10. Golden leaves cover the trees.

Notes for Home: Your child identified the subjects and predicates of sentences. ***Home Activity:*** Read a folk tale with your child and encourage him or her to point out the subjects and predicates in some of the sentences.

Name ______________________________

Subjects and Predicates

Directions: Unscramble each group of words to make a complete sentence. Write the subject on the single line. Write the predicate on the double line. Remember to use capital letters and end marks.

1. eat breakfast together | likes to | my family

______________ ══════════════════

2. cooks oatmeal | my grandmother | for us

______________ ══════════════════

3. with raisins | oatmeal | tastes delicious

______________ ══════════════════

4. likes | our whole family | hot cereal

______________ ══════════════════

5. two helpings | my sister | can eat

______________ ══════════════════

Directions: Write a subject or predicate to complete each sentence.

6. ______________________ enjoys eating breakfast outdoors.

7. ______________________ will keep the sun off.

8. I ______________________.

9. ______________________ sometimes barks for food.

10. My favorite breakfast ______________________.

Write a Journal Entry

On a separate sheet of paper, write about a family breakfast you remember. Then mark the subject and predicate in each sentence you wrote.

Notes for Home: Your child practiced using subjects and predicates to write sentences. ***Home Activity:*** Read a funny story with your child. Point to easy sentences and encourage your child to identify the subjects and predicates.

Name ______________________________

Subjects and Predicates

RETEACHING

Read the sentence. Then write the word that tells who the sentence is about.

Tanya ate an apple.

1. ______________________________ (subject)

Write the words that tell what Tanya did.

2. ______________________________ (predicate)

A sentence has two parts. The **subject** names someone or something. The **predicate** tells what the subject is or does. The subject and predicate of a sentence must make sense together.

Directions: Circle **subject** if the subject is underlined. Circle **predicate** if the predicate is underlined.

1. <u>Americans</u> moved west. subject predicate

2. John Chapman <u>took apple seeds to Ohio.</u> subject predicate

3. <u>He</u> planted the seeds near streams. subject predicate

4. Many people <u>called him Johnny Appleseed.</u> subject predicate

5. The trees <u>grew throughout the Middle West.</u> subject predicate

Directions: Write the subject of each sentence.

6. The happy girl found the trees. ____________________

7. She ate red and green apples. ____________________

8. Her brother climbed the tree. ____________________

9. He put the apples in his pocket. ____________________

Notes for Home: Your child identified subjects and predicates in sentences. ***Home Activity:*** Together, look at one page of a favorite book. Have your child make up new sentences using subjects of three sentences on that page.

Name ____________________

Subjects and Predicates

Directions: Draw one line under the subject in each sentence. Draw two lines under the predicate.

1. Young people learn about their country from dolls.
2. Old dolls traveled by wagon to the American West.
3. Sailors carve dolls from bone.
4. My favorite doll opens and shuts its eyes.
5. Some workers fix broken dolls.

Directions: Draw a line to match each subject with a predicate that makes the most sense. Then write the complete sentences.

Subjects	**Predicates**
Small buttons	buys interesting dolls.
A doll collector	play with soft dolls.
Young children	is a famous doll.
Raggedy Ann	can become eyes for dolls.

6. ____________________
7. ____________________
8. ____________________
9. ____________________

Write a Story

Write a story about a doll or toy you own. Be sure each sentence has a subject and a predicate. Write on a separate sheet of paper.

Notes for Home: Your.child identified subjects and predicates and wrote complete sentences. ***Home Activity:*** Write sentences on strips of paper and use scissors to cut them between the subject and predicate. Have your child put the sentences back together.

Name ______________________________

Subjects and Predicates

REVIEW

Directions: Underline the subject of each sentence.

1. Barrel racing is one very exciting rodeo sport.

2. Rodeo hands set three big barrels in the rodeo ring.

3. When do the expert horsewomen ride into the ring?

4. What path does each rider follow?

5. The horse and rider must circle each barrel.

Directions: Underline the predicate of each sentence.

6. The racers gallop back to the starting line.

7. How does a rider win first prize?

8. All the swift riders cut very close to the barrels.

9. This takes seconds off their scores.

10. They try to clear all the barrels.

Directions: Write a subject or predicate to complete each sentence.

11. ______________________________ is my favorite rodeo event.

12. ______________________________ is the rider with the fastest time.

13. ______________________________ are very well trained.

14. The best horses ______________________________.

15. The slowest racer ______________________________.

Notes for Home: Your child identified and wrote subjects (the words that tell who or what does the action) and predicates (the words that tell the action). ***Home Activity:*** Circle a simple sentence in a newspaper story. Have your child identify the subject and the predicate.

Name ______________________________

Statements and Questions

A **statement** is a sentence that tells something. It ends with a period.

I like riding horses.

A **question** is a sentence that asks something. It ends with a question mark.

Do you like riding horses?

Directions: Decide whether each sentence is a statement or a question. Circle the correct punctuation mark for the end of each sentence.

1. Have you ever ridden a horse . ?

2. Last summer I rode a horse at the fair . ?

3. It must have been ten feet high . ?

4. Anyway, the ground looked far away . ?

5. Can I get off now . ?

Directions: Rewrite each sentence so that it begins with a capital letter and ends with the correct punctuation.

6. riding a horse isn't as much fun as it looks

____

7. have you ever been on a very rocky road

____

8. it feels like riding a bike over rocks

____

9. can new riders control their horses

____

10. no, horses sometimes have minds of their own

____

Notes for Home: Your child used periods and question marks to write statements and questions. ***Home Activity:*** Together, try to remember an outdoor experience you both enjoyed. Challenge one another's memory by writing questions for the other person to answer with a statement.

Name ________________________________

Statements and Questions

Directions: Read each sentence. Write **S** on the line if it is a statement. Write **Q** if it is a question. Rewrite each sentence correctly in the speech bubble in the picture.

________ **1.** what is that

2.

________ **3.** this is my charro hat

4.

________ **5.** can I wear it

6.

________ **7.** it is too big for you

8.

________ **9.** no, it is not too big

10.

Write Dialogue for a Comic Strip

On a separate sheet of paper, draw your own comic strip. Use at least five complete sentences in the speech bubbles. Make two of them questions.

Notes for Home: Your child wrote statements and questions, using capital letters and a period or question mark. ***Home Activity:*** Work with your child to draw a two-box comic strip which has one character asking a question and another character answering it.

Name ______________________________

Statements and Questions

RETEACHING

Read the riddle below.

1. Why did Silly Sam go to bed on the lamp? _____

2. He was a light sleeper. _____

Write an **X** after the sentence that tells something. This sentence is a statement. Write a check after the sentence that asks something. This sentence is a question.

A **statement** is a sentence that tells something. It ends with a period. A **question** is a sentence that asks something. It ends with a question mark. All sentences begin with capital letters.

Directions: Fill in each blank with the proper end mark: a period or a question mark.

1. Where does a lamb go to get a haircut _____

It goes to the Baa Baa Shop _____

2. Some riddles are funny _____ Do you laugh at riddles _____

3. These riddles are silly _____ Can you tell me more _____

Directions: Unscramble each word group below. Add a question mark if the words form a question. Add a period if they form a statement.

4. riddles book is a Here of

____

5. Do riddles you new like

____

Notes for Home: Your child identified and completed statements and questions, using correct punctuation. ***Home Activity:*** Look at a story and talk about end punctuation for statements and questions. Have your child read sentences and identify the end punctuation.

Name ______________________________

Statements and Questions

Directions: On each line of the detective's notepad, write a question about a classmate. Then fold the page to write the answers. Remember: A **statement** begins with a capital letter and ends with a period. A **question** begins with a capital letter and ends with a question mark.

DETECTIVES, INC.

QUESTIONS:

1.

2.

3.

ANSWERS:

1.

2.

3.

Directions: When you're finished, exchange papers with a classmate. Have him or her try to answer all the questions before peeking at the answer key.

Notes for Home: Your child wrote questions and statements, using capital letters and a period or question mark. ***Home Activity:*** Have your child write two questions and your responses. Make sure your child uses capital letters and correct end punctuation.

Name ______________________________

Statements and Questions

REVIEW

Directions: Read each sentence. Write **S** on the line if it is a statement. Write **Q** if it is a question.

_______________ **1.** Have you ever had chicken pox?

_______________ **2.** Did you catch it from someone else?

_______________ **3.** It's easy to pass chicken pox from person to person.

_______________ **4.** This disease spreads fast because children may not know they have it.

_______________ **5.** Why is that?

_______________ **6.** They don't break out in spots until two or three weeks after they catch it.

_______________ **7.** What are the first signs of chicken pox?

_______________ **8.** You may get a headache and a fever.

_______________ **9.** What if I see a red rash on my chest?

_______________ **10.** A rash is another sign of chicken pox.

Directions: Read each sentence. Add the correct end punctuation.

11. If you get chicken pox once, you usually won't get it again _____

12. Did you know that there is a new shot that keeps you from getting chicken pox _____

13. Does the shot hurt _____

14. Many shots can keep people from getting certain diseases for the rest of their lives _____

15. That is why most people get shots when they are children _____

Notes for Home: Your child identified statements and questions and punctuated them. ***Home Activity:*** Watch a TV interview with your child. Have him or her identify statements and questions in the conversation.

Name ______________________________

Commands and Exclamations

A **command** is a sentence that tells someone to do something. Some commands begin with *please*. Commands usually end with periods.

Please get me some orange juice.

An **exclamation** is a sentence that shows strong feelings, such as anger, surprise, fear, or excitement. It ends with an exclamation mark.

I feel so awful!

Directions: Circle the punctuation mark at the end of each sentence. Then write **C** if the sentence is a command. Write **E** if it is an exclamation.

________ **1.** What a terrible cold you have!

________ **2.** Stay in bed until you're well.

________ **3.** Drink this glass of juice.

________ **4.** Your forehead is really hot!

________ **5.** Try to eat a little soup.

Directions: Decide whether each sentence is a command or exclamation. Then rewrite it on the line. Be sure to use a capital letter at the beginning and the correct end punctuation.

6. what a mess the bed is ______________________________

7. help me smooth out the sheets ______________________________

8. oh no, you dropped your pillow ______________________________

9. please climb back into bed ______________________________

10. go to sleep ______________________________

Notes for Home: Your child identified and wrote commands and exclamations, using periods and exclamation marks. ***Home Activity:*** Challenge your child to make up three commands and to express different emotions with three exclamations.

Name ________________________________

Commands and Exclamations

Directions: Think about what the children in each picture might be saying. Follow the directions for each picture.

1. Write an exclamation in the big sister's speech balloon.
2. What punctuation mark did you use? ____________________
3. Write a command in the boy's speech balloon.
4. What punctuation mark did you use? ____________________

5. Write an exclamation or a command in the boy's speech balloon.

Write a Get-Well Note

On a separate sheet of paper, write a note to a friend who is sick. Use one exclamation and two commands in your note.

Notes for Home: Your child wrote commands and exclamations. ***Home Activity:*** Suggest that your child imagine being a doctor. Encourage your child to think of some commands and exclamations he or she might use when speaking with a patient.

Name ______________________________

Commands and Exclamations

RETEACHING

Write a sentence. Tell the boy in the picture to go get his raincoat. Use a period as the end mark.

1. ______________________________

Write a sentence about wearing a raincoat. Use an exclamation mark to show strong feeling.

2. ______________________________

A **command** is a sentence that tells someone to do something. It ends with a period. An **exclamation** is a sentence that shows strong feeling. It ends with an exclamation mark.

Directions: Each sentence below is a command or an exclamation. Fill in the blank with a period or an exclamation mark.

1. I'm so happy ______

2. Bring your sister ______

3. What fun it is ______

4. Call me soon ______

Directions: Circle each exclamation. Write it correctly.

5. i love this wrapping paper take off the ribbon

____

6. that is my favorite book pass the book around

____

7. say good-bye to everyone the party was so much fun

____

Notes for Home: Your child used correct end punctuation for commands and exclamations. ***Home Activity:*** Have your child imagine visiting a famous place and write about the visit, using at least one command and one exclamation.

Name ______________________________

Commands and Exclamations

Directions: Write a period or an exclamation mark after each sentence. Then write **command** or **exclamation**.

1. I can't wait to start the treasure hunt ______ ________________
2. I am so excited ______ ________________
3. Study the treasure map ______ ________________
4. Start at the red brick house ______ ________________

Directions: Write each command and exclamation correctly. Use a capital letter and the correct end mark.

5. ____
6. ____
7. ____
8. ____

Write a Poem

Write a poem about a time when you found something special. Include both an exclamation and a command. Write on a separate sheet of paper.

Notes for Home: Your child identified and wrote commands and exclamations. ***Home Activity:*** Together, create a three-box comic strip. Have your child write commands and exclamations for the comic-strip characters to say.

Name ____________________________________

Commands and Exclamations

REVIEW

Directions: Read each sentence. Write **C** if the sentence is a command. Write **E** if it is an exclamation.

________ **1.** What a cool board game!

________ **2.** Come and play it with me.

________ **3.** I'm a terrible player!

________ **4.** Practice playing it more often.

________ **5.** Please sit down here and choose your game piece.

Directions: Read each sentence. Add the correct end punctuation.

6. This robot is great _____

7. That robot is mine _____

8. Choose a game piece _____

9. This game is really fun _____

10. Teach me the rules _____

11. Just spin this spinner _____

12. Pick a direction _____

13. I win _____

Directions: Write a command and an exclamation on the lines below.

14. ____

15. ____

Notes for Home: Your child identified commands and exclamations and punctuated them with periods and exclamation marks. ***Home Activity:*** Challenge your child to write three commands and three exclamations that might be heard at a ball game. Check punctuation for each sentence.

Clear and Interesting Subjects

Many sentences need only one word as the subject.

Rita is my sister. She plays basketball very well.

Other sentences give more information in a subject that has a number of words.

My other sister, Lu, taught us how to play.

The best player in town taught Lu.

When you write, use subjects that will interest readers and give clear information. Good subjects can be short or long.

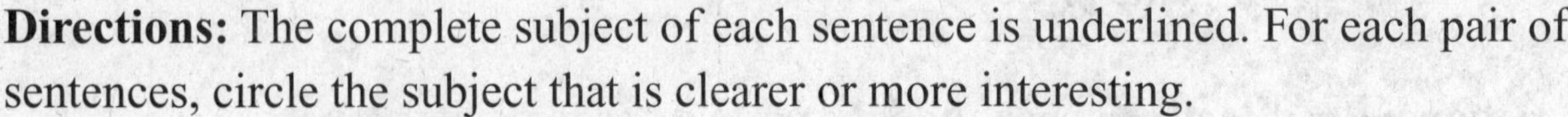

Directions: The complete subject of each sentence is underlined. For each pair of sentences, circle the subject that is clearer or more interesting.

1. We played the Wildcats.

   Our basketball team played the Wildcats.

2. The championship game was at three o'clock.

   It was at three o'clock.

3. Our shortest player scored first.

   Someone on our team scored first.

4. Her name is Mary.

   What we call her when we talk is Mary.

5. The Wildcats' fastest player shot the next basket.

   He shot the next basket.

6. It was tied.

   The game was tied.

7. Can you guess what happened next?

   Can someone or other guess what happened next?

8. My new hero quickly dribbled the ball to the basket.

   Somebody quickly dribbled the ball to the basket.

9. My relative is the hero.

   My sister Rita is the hero.

10. Her many baskets won the game for us.

    What she did won the game for us.

Notes for Home: Your child identified clear and interesting subjects of sentences. ***Home Activity:*** Read some of the sentences in a book or magazine with your child. Ask which sentence subjects seemed clearest or most interesting to your child.

Name ______________________________

Clear and Interesting Subjects

Directions: The complete subject of each sentence is underlined. For each pair of sentences, circle the subject that is clearer or more interesting.

1. He invented basketball in 1891.

A college professor invented basketball in 1891.

2. The students in his class exercised indoors in winter.

They exercised indoors in winter.

3. Their gym exercises seemed very dull to them.

Those things that they did seemed very dull to them

4. Dr. Naismith invented an active indoor game called basketball.

That man I was talking about invented an active indoor game called basketball.

5. This exciting new sport could be played in winter and at night.

It could be played in winter and at night.

Directions: Replace the underlined subject of each sentence with a more clear or interesting subject. Write the subject on the line.

6. That sport with the orange ball is my favorite sport. ______________

7. The place where I go to learn has a great team. ______________

8. We practice everyday. ______________

9. The man who coaches us played college basketball. ______________

10. This game is a lot of fun. ______________

Write a Sportscast

Write what a sportscaster watching an exciting basketball game might say. Use clear or interesting subjects. Underline each subject.

Notes for Home: Your child identified and wrote clear and interesting subjects of sentences. ***Home Activity:*** Practice writing sentences with your child that use clear and interesting subjects.

Name ____________________

RETEACHING

Clear and Interesting Subjects

Read the sentences. Circle the sentence with the clearer or more interesting subject, and underline the subject.

1. The time in the day before afternoon is the most beautiful.
2. The morning is the most beautiful.

Use subjects that will give clear information and will interest readers.

Directions: Read the subjects in the box. Then read each sentence below. The subject of each sentence is underlined. Choose a clearer or more interesting subject from the box and write it on the line.

desk	my cousin David	my pencils, pens, and markers
my neighbor Mrs. Jonas	fire alarm	

1. Today the woman who lives in the apartment near mine took me to school.

   ____

2. The boy who is my father's sister's son gave me a warning before I went inside the classroom. ____________________
3. My seat in class had been knocked over! ____________________
4. Those objects I write and draw with were rolling across the floor.

   ____

5. The sudden, loud noise went off before I could clean up. ____________________

Directions:

6–7. Write two sentences with clear and interesting subjects on a separate sheet of paper. Exchange papers with a classmate and talk about why you chose your subjects.

Notes for Home: Your child used clear and interesting subjects in sentences. ***Home Activity:*** Say a sentence. (For example: *That animal chewed on a shoe.*) Ask your child to repeat it, using a clearer or more interesting subject. *(Our dog chewed on a shoe.)*

Clear and Interesting Subjects

Directions: Circle the subject of each sentence. Rewrite each sentence, using a clear and interesting subject.

1. That boy raced across the yard.

____

2. Some paper with writing on it was in his hand.

____

3. The things on his feet made no sound as he ran through the grass.

____

4. What he talks and eats with opened in a big grin.

____

5. The younger boy in his family asked him why he was so happy.

____

6. The boy that was running held open his hand.

____

7. His mother's mother had written him a letter and sent something else too.

____

____

8. A picture was also in the envelope.

____

9. "Everyone can finally see Grandma and Grandpa's new house!"

____

____

Notes for Home: Your child rewrote sentences, using clear and interesting subjects. ***Home Activity:*** Look at family pictures or pictures in magazines or newspapers. Take turns describing the pictures, using sentences with clear and interesting subjects.

Name ________________________________

Subjects

REVIEW

Directions: Underline the subject in each sentence.

1. My big brother Randy likes to collect plants.
2. Randy buys a new plant almost every week.
3. His collection of plants is very large.
4. The teacher asked Randy to bring one to school.
5. Randy wins a prize for his plants every year.
6. My hobby is very different from Randy's.
7. I collect stamps.
8. The third and fourth grade students have a stamp club.
9. All the stamp collectors meet once a month.
10. The stamp clubs in other schools meet with us too.

Directions: Add a subject to complete each sentence. Write the sentence on the line.

11. _____ likes to work in the garden.

____

12. _____ grows both vegetables and flowers.

____

13. _____ are two of the loveliest flowers in the garden.

____

14. _____ picks corn and tomatoes in September.

____

15. _____ are delicious.

____

Notes for Home: Your child identified and wrote subjects—words that tell who or what does the action—in sentences. ***Home Activity:*** Read a story with your child. Encourage your child to find the subjects in several sentences.

Nouns

A **noun** is a word that names a person, a place, or a thing.

The gardener grows special plants in his garden.

Directions: One noun in each sentence is underlined. Find and underline the other nouns in the sentence.

1. There are some plants that use animals as food.
2. They also make their own food using air and sunshine, just like other plants.
3. They grow in swamps and marshes or in soil that has few minerals.
4. Food and minerals from animals help plants to live and grow.
5. How do plants get flies, ants, mice, frogs, and even birds?
6. The color, smell, or nectar on the plant brings animals.
7. Leaves are often very special traps on carnivorous plants.
8. The deep, slippery pitcher plants can catch insects, lizards, frogs, and birds.
9. The Venus flytrap has leaves with teeth that snap together.
10. Small ants can sometimes crawl out, but a fly will not escape.
11. The butterwort has sticky gum on its leaves.
12. When a spider crawls onto the leaf, it sticks to the gum.
13. The spider tries to get away, but the leaf makes more of the sticky gum.
14. The leaf curls up, and juices pour out to digest the spider.
15. Later, the leaf slowly opens and makes more gum to catch another animal!

Notes for Home: Your child identified nouns—words that name people, places, and things—in sentences. ***Home Activity:*** Together, read several sentences from a book or a magazine. Challenge your child to name one noun in each sentence.

Name ______________________________

Nouns

Directions: Circle the nouns in the box. Use them to complete the puzzle. Each noun will fit in one place in the puzzle. Some words have been started for you.

insect	see	snail	walks
grass	plant	pretty	frog
goldfish	lizard	food	grows
ironed	sun	raindrop	five
leaned	picky	bald	tree

Write a Journal Entry

How would you feel if you were a fly landing on a Venus flytrap? What would you see? What would you expect to happen? On a separate sheet of paper, write a journal entry that might be written by that fly. When you're done, go back and underline all the nouns in the entry.

Notes for Home: Your child identified nouns—words that name people, places, or things. ***Home Activity:*** Find a household object that has writing on it, such as a food package or a videotape box. Challenge your child to identify all the nouns.

Name ____________________________________

Nouns

RETEACHING

Complete each sentence. Write the noun **farmer**, **farm**, or **potatoes**. Use each clue in ( ) to help you.

1. I am a ____________________ . (names a person)

2. I live on a ____________________ . (names a place)

3. I like ____________________ . (names a thing)

Nouns name persons, places, or things.

Directions: Write each noun. Use the words from the list.

sister	sell	dog	barn	field	sharpen
carry	country	fence	driver	cow	wheat

1. __________________ **4.** __________________ **7.** __________________

2. __________________ **5.** __________________ **8.** __________________

3. __________________ **6.** __________________ **9.** __________________

Directions: Complete each sentence. Write the correct noun from the box.

man	pie	vegetable	family	basket	village

10. A __________________ opened the car door.

11. He held a __________________ of potatoes.

12. I live in the next __________________ .

13. My __________________ will have a surprise for dinner.

14. I will bake a pumpkin __________________ tonight.

15. Potatoes are my favorite __________________ .

Notes for Home: Your child identified and wrote nouns—words that name persons, places, or things. ***Home Activity:*** Talk with your child about the people, places, and things each of you has seen today.

Nouns

Directions: Write your name and your friend's name on the blanks and then complete each sentence with a noun. Remember: A **noun** is a word that names a person, place, or thing.

1. __________ (You) : I'm hungry. Let's eat some **2.** __________ (noun) !

3. __________ (Your Friend) : How about some fresh **4.** __________ (noun) ?

5. __________ (You) : That's boring! Let's find something we both like to eat in the kitchen. How about a **6.** __________ (noun) ?

Dog : WOOF! WOOF!

Cat : MEOW!

7. __________ (Your Friend) : HELP! It looks like we have some hungry friends. Let's distract them by taking them to the **8.** __________ (noun) .

9. __________ (You) : What a great idea! After that we can go to the **10.** __________ (noun) !

11. __________ (Your Friend) : We can go to a **12.** __________ (noun) there!

13. __________ (You) : Great! I'll bring a **14.** __________ (noun) too!

Notes for Home: Your child wrote nouns—words that name persons, places, and things. ***Home Activity:*** Help your child cut out pictures from magazines or newspapers, and have your child label the pictures with nouns.

Name ______________________________

Nouns

REVIEW

Directions: Underline the noun or nouns in each sentence.

1. The girls from space landed in my yard.

2. They asked me to go for a ride in their spaceship.

3. I asked my father if I could go.

4. He said I had to be home in time for lunch.

5. The girls from space told me that I needed a spacesuit.

6. I put on some overalls that my brother had outgrown.

7. We got in the spaceship and sat in chairs that had many buttons.

8. We flew to another planet.

9. I saw many strange creatures and weird buildings.

10. One creature gave me a sandwich with peanut butter, but no jelly.

Directions: Add a subject or a predicate to complete each sentence. Write the sentence on the line. Then underline all the nouns in each sentence.

11. I _____.

____

12. _____ had never heard of a sandwich with jelly.

____

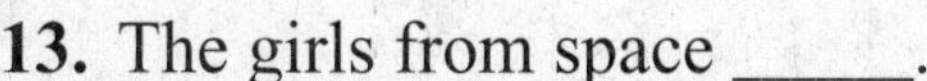

13. The girls from space _____.

____

14. _____ wanted to tell all their friends.

____

15. Their friends _____.

____

Notes for Home: Your child identified nouns in sentences. ***Home Activity:*** Read aloud sentences from a book, one word at a time. Have your child raise his or her hand for each noun.

Name ____________________

Nouns in Sentences

A **noun** can be the main word in the subject of a sentence.

The huge spaceship landed.

Nouns can also appear in other parts of a sentence.

The pilot opened the door slowly.

The huge spaceship landed on the moon.

Directions: The subject of each sentence is underlined. Draw a circle around the noun or nouns in the simple subject of each sentence.

1. Many books have been written about space beings.
2. Some people believed that there were creatures on the moon.
3. Both adults and children wondered if people would ever travel to the moon.
4. Some brave astronauts did visit the moon.
5. The men found no living plants or animals.

Directions: The noun in each subject is underlined. Draw a circle around the other noun or nouns in each sentence.

6. Astronauts have not yet visited more distant planets.
7. Several probes have taken pictures of planets in space.
8. Many scientists study this information to find out more about these planets.
9. Mars has a surface that looks red from Earth.
10. Saturn is a planet that has many rings around it.
11. Pluto is the smallest planet in our system and the farthest from the Sun.
12. Can other life be found beyond Earth?
13. Do any other planets have air and water?
14. Some planets are very cold and have poison in the air.
15. Earth is the only planet with plants and animals!

Notes for Home: Your child identified the nouns—words that name persons, places, or things—in sentences. ***Home Activity:*** Ask your child to write sentences with two nouns in the subject—the sentence part that tells who or what the sentence is about.

Name ____

Nouns in Sentences

Directions: Underline the noun or nouns in the subject of each sentence. If there are any nouns in the rest of the sentence, circle them.

1. Latesha is my big sister.
2. Latesha wants to be an astronaut.
3. My sister will have to pass a very tough test to become an astronaut.
4. Our mother says Latesha is tough too.
5. Our father agrees.
6. Our father says Latesha will pass all the tests.
7. Latesha studies science almost every day.
8. Many astronauts are scientists.
9. Latesha and her friends swim laps at the pool every day.
10. A person has to be fit in order to be an astronaut.

Directions: Choose a noun to complete each sentence. Write the noun on the line to the left.

____________________ **11.** I built a spaceship in my _____.

____________________ **12.** It looked like a _____.

____________________ **13.** I flew my spaceship to _____.

____________________ **14.** My _____ went with me.

____________________ **15.** The _____ met us when we landed.

Write a Newspaper Article

Your homemade spaceship has just returned from space. On a separate sheet of paper, write an article describing what happened at the landing site. When you're done, underline all the nouns you used.

Notes for Home: Your child identified nouns in sentences. ***Home Activity:*** Ask your child to name an event that happened in your home today. Challenge your child to write three sentences about the event. Each sentence should have at least two nouns in it.

Nouns in Sentences

RETEACHING

A line is drawn after the subject of each sentence.
Complete each subject with a word from the box.

logs
boats
children
tires

1. The ____________________ | float in the lake.

2. Two happy ____________________ | float in the lake.

The subject of a sentence names someone or something. The main word in the subject of a sentence often is a noun.

Directions: The subject is underlined in each sentence. Circle the noun in each subject. Then circle any other nouns in each sentence.

1. <u>Many boats</u> are tied along the dock.
2. <u>A woman</u> hops into a small boat.
3. <u>A boy</u> unties the knot.
4. <u>White sails</u> go up.
5. <u>The wind</u> pushes the sails.
6. <u>Some puffy clouds</u> float in the sky.

Directions: Complete each sentence with a noun. Write a noun from the box.

day	people	sailor	ducks

7. The ____________________ is warm and sunny.

8. A ____________________ steers the boat.

9. A few ____________________ watch from the dock.

10. They see ____________________ behind the boat.

Notes for Home: Your child identified nouns—words that name people, places, and things—and used them in sentences. ***Home Activity:*** Read a favorite story together and have your child make up new sentences with nouns from the story.

Name ________________________________

Nouns in Sentences

Directions: The subject or another phrase is underlined in each sentence. Circle the noun.

1. Some fish swim in a big tank.
2. A tall boy watches their fins.
3. Two parrots chatter loudly.
4. Three yellow canaries sing the same song.
5. A small kitten meows softly.
6. The store has many good pets for children.

Directions: The noun in each subject is underlined. Change this noun to a different noun. Write a new sentence.

7. Four puppies play in the store window.

____

8. Many people look at them.

____

9. Two girls walk into the pet store.

____

10. A small kitten sleeps in a corner.

____

11. A rabbit nibbles its food.

____

Write a Story

Write a story about a pet store. Then circle an important noun in each sentence. Write on a separate sheet of paper.

Notes for Home: Your child used nouns—words that name people, places, and things—in sentences. ***Home Activity:*** Make a list of nouns together, and then have your child write sentences using these nouns.

Name ______________________________________

Nouns in Sentences

REVIEW

Directions: Underline the subject in each sentence. Circle the noun or nouns in each subject.

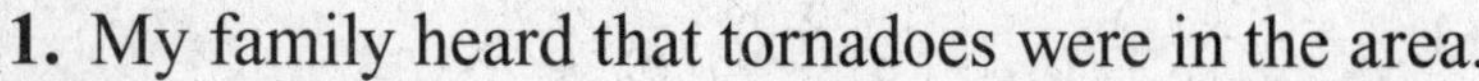

1. My family heard that tornadoes were in the area.
2. My father went down to check our storm cellar.
3. My grandmother and grandfather gathered food and a radio.
4. My brother and sister looked for tornadoes across the field.
5. Our neighbors had heard about the tornadoes too.

Directions: Underline the predicate in each sentence. Circle the noun or nouns in each predicate.

6. We couldn't spot any tornadoes.
7. My sister and I brought our two dogs inside the house.
8. Then my mother called my father on the telephone.
9. We all watched the news on television.
10. The reporter had good news.

Directions: Write a noun to complete each sentence. Add other words if needed.

________________ **11.** _____ were no longer in the area.

________________ **12.** Our family had a little _____ to celebrate.

________________ **13.** Then my brother, sister, and I watched a funny _____.

________________ **14.** Later we ate some delicious _____.

________________ **15.** Finally _____ was ready for bed.

Notes for Home: Your child identified and wrote nouns in subjects and predicates of sentences. ***Home Activity:*** Go on a noun treasure hunt. Make a list of people, places, or things in or near your home. Take turns writing sentences using these nouns.

Name ______________________________

Singular and Plural Nouns

A noun that names only one person, place, or thing is called a **singular noun**. A noun that names more than one is called a **plural noun**.

Add **-s** to form the plural of most nouns: **raindrops.**
Add **-es** to form the plural of nouns that end in **ch, sh, s, ss,** or **x: branches, foxes.**
To form the plural of nouns that end in a consonant and **y,** change the **y** to **i** and add **-es: parties.**

Some plural nouns do not follow a regular pattern. You will need to remember these **irregular nouns: men, children, mice, deer.**

Directions: Write the plural of each singular noun.

1. cloud ______________

2. tulip ______________

3. box ______________

4. beach ______________

5. home ______________

6. wish ______________

7. lady ______________

8. cyclone ______________

9. funnel ______________

10. woman ______________

11. class ______________

12. storm ______________

13. tray ______________

14. baby ______________

15. twister ______________

16. hailstone ______________

Directions: Circle the noun in ( ) that best completes each sentence.

17. All the (child/children) at our school went to the science museum.

18. We ate our boxed (lunch/lunches) in the museum cafeteria.

19. Then we saw two (movie/movies) that showed what tornadoes have done.

20. They have destroyed whole towns and parts of (city/cities).

Notes for Home: Your child noted the difference between singular and plural nouns. ***Home Activity:*** Work with your child to list objects in the room. Ask your child to identify the singular and plural nouns on the list.

Name ______________________________

Singular and Plural Nouns

Directions: Write the singular or plural form of the noun in ( ) to complete each sentence.

______________ **1.** A tornado (watch) told us the storm was coming.

______________ **2.** As the wind grew stronger, many of the (tree) began to sway and bend.

______________ **3.** When we heard the first tornado (warning), we knew it was time to take shelter.

______________ **4.** A neighbor and his three (child) came over to stay in our basement.

______________ **5.** We had lots of (supply), such as water, candles, and batteries, ready.

______________ **6.** After just a few (minute), we heard the loud roar of the tornado.

______________ **7.** It seemed like many (hour) before we could leave the basement.

______________ **8.** Strong winds had damaged many (home) around us.

______________ **9.** Some trees lost lots of (branch) and others were uprooted.

______________ **10.** Many (day) later, we still had lots to clean up.

Write a Television News Report

Imagine that you're a TV news reporter. You're doing a story on a tornado that hit your town today. Camera crews have filmed the damage. On a separate sheet of paper, write a news report describing what's on the film. Be sure to use several singular nouns as well as several plural nouns.

Notes for Home: Your child wrote sentences with singular and plural nouns. ***Home Activity:*** Ask your child to point out the nouns in newspaper headlines and to say whether they are singular or plural.

Name ____________________

Singular and Plural Nouns

RETEACHING

Circle each noun that names things in the picture.

Singular Nouns	Plural Nouns
shell	shells
shovel	shovels
pail	pails

A **singular noun** names one person, place, or thing. A **plural noun** names more than one person, place, or thing. Add **-s** to form the plural of most nouns.

Directions: Circle **singular** if the noun is singular. Circle **plural** if the noun is plural.

1. tents	singular	plural	**4.** buckets	singular	plural
2. crab	singular	plural	**5.** pigeons	singular	plural
3. gulls	singular	plural	**6.** chair	singular	plural

Directions: A singular noun is underlined in each sentence pair. Write the plural form of each underlined noun.

7. The <u>wave</u> hits the beach.

The ____________________ hit the beach.

8. My mother builds a <u>castle</u> in the sand.

My mother builds ____________________ in the sand.

9. I test the water with my <u>toe</u>.

I test the water with my ____________________.

Notes for Home: Your child identified nouns as singular or plural. ***Home Activity:*** Read a favorite story together and challenge your child to make a list of singular and plural nouns from the story.

Singular and Plural Nouns

Directions: Underline the singular noun in each sentence. Circle the plural noun.

1. Trucks stop in front of the store.

2. The drivers deliver food.

3. A woman opens the doors.

4. The jars go on each shelf.

Directions: Complete the puzzle. Write the plural form of each noun in ( ). Start the first word in square 5.

5. A woman buys three red ______. (apple)

6. She checks both ______ in her hands. (list)

7. Two ______ of soup fall to the floor. (can)

8. A girl wants some ______. (peanut)

9. A boy packs the food in ______. (bag)

5

6

7

8

9

Write a Paragraph

Write a paragraph about a trip to a market. Use both singular and plural nouns to name persons, places, and things. Write on a separate sheet of paper.

Notes for Home: Your child identified and used plural nouns—words that name more than one person, place, or thing. ***Home Activity:*** Have your child use singular (one) and plural (more than one) nouns to create labels for items in your home.

Name ______________________

Singular and Plural Nouns

REVIEW

Directions: Read each sentence. Write **S** on the line if the underlined noun is singular. Write **P** on the line if it is plural.

_______ **1.** A glacier is a huge mass of ice.

_______ **2.** Ocean waves may crack the glacier.

_______ **3.** A piece of ice may break off to make an iceberg.

_______ **4.** An iceberg may look like many boxes piled together.

_______ **5.** It may look like a row of pointy teeth.

_______ **6.** Several icebergs can form an ice pack.

_______ **7.** Ice packs look like floating cities of ice.

_______ **8.** Small parts of an iceberg may break off.

_______ **9.** People may see only the top of an iceberg.

_______ **10.** The bottom is below the water's surface.

Directions: Use the plural form of each noun below in a sentence. Write the sentence on the line.

passenger	ship	family	iceberg	child

11. ______________________

12. ______________________

13. ______________________

14. ______________________

15. ______________________

Notes for Home: Your child identified singular and plural nouns. ***Home Activity:*** Play a noun game with your child. Toss a coin. If the coin lands "heads," your child says a singular noun. If the coin lands "tails," your child says a plural noun.

Name ___________________________________

Possessive Nouns

A noun that shows ownership is a **possessive noun**. Add an **apostrophe (')** and **-s** to a singular noun to make it possessive.

dog **dog's** dish

Add an **apostrophe (')** to a plural noun that ends in **-s, -es,** or **-ies** to make it possessive.

girls **girls'** team

Add an **apostrophe (')** and **-s,** to make other plural nouns possessive.

children **children's** toys

Directions: Add **('s)** or **(')** to each word to form the possessive.

1. Billy ____ room

2. teachers ____ meeting

3. children ____ lunchboxes

4. foxes ____ cage

5. cousins ____ house

6. mayor ____ office

7. cars ____ horns

8. babies ____ books

9. bird ____ nest

10. animals ____ tracks

Directions: Use the possessive form of the noun in ( ) to complete each sentence. Write the possessive noun on the line.

________________ **11.** We sailed along (Alaska) coast to see glaciers and icebergs.

________________ **12.** It was our (family) first trip to Alaska.

________________ **13.** When the (ocean) waves beat against a glacier, large chunks break off.

________________ **14.** The (icebergs) tops are all that people can see.

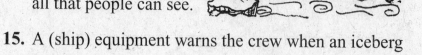

________________ **15.** A (ship) equipment warns the crew when an iceberg is near.

Notes for Home: Your child wrote the possessive form of singular nouns and plural nouns to show ownership. ***Home Activity:*** Play a noun game with your child. Name a noun and ask your child to write or spell the word as a possessive noun.

Possessive Nouns

Directions: Write the possessive form of the underlined noun.

1. the book by the author — the __________ book
2. a hat belonging to the man — the __________ hat
3. the toys belonging to the babies — the __________ toys
4. pens belonging to the students — the __________ pens
5. the tops of the boxes — the __________ tops
6. a dress belonging to the woman — the __________ dress
7. the librarian who works for the school — the __________ librarian
8. bikes belonging to the boys — the __________ bikes
9. the car belonging to my parents — my __________ car
10. the animals that are owned by the zoo — the __________ animals
11. the voices of the singers — the __________ voices
12. the program for the children — the __________ program
13. the engines of the planes — the __________ engines
14. boots belonging to the hikers — the __________ boots
15. passengers on the ships — the __________ passengers

Write a Ship's Log

A ship's crew keeps a log. A log is like a journal. It describes what happened on the ship on each day of the trip. Imagine you were on a ship and saw icebergs. On a separate sheet of paper, write a paragraph from that ship's log. Include possessive nouns in your paragraph.

Notes for Home: Your child wrote possessive forms of singular and plural nouns to show ownership. ***Home Activity:*** Ask your child to name things in your home that belong to someone or something (For example: *the cat's dish* or *your brothers' room*).

Possessive Nouns

RETEACHING

Match each word group on the left to one on the right that has the same meaning. Draw a line to connect the word groups.

1. the tails of the cats	Jan's toy
2. the toy that belongs to Jan	the cats' tails

Nouns name persons, places, or things. A **possessive noun** shows ownership. To form the possessive form of a **singular noun**, add an apostrophe and **-s ('s)**. To form the possessive form of a **plural noun** that ends in **-s**, add an apostrophe (').

Directions: Circle the possessive noun in each sentence. Then write it on the line.

1. Mr. Flint's class made toy animals. ______________

2. Jenny's toy is a green parrot. ______________

3. The parrots' eyes are orange. ______________

4. Miko's elephants are funny. ______________

5. Miko put the dresses on the elephants' bodies. ______________

Directions: Rewrite each sentence below. Use the possessive form of the underlined noun.

6. The spider web was made of string.

____

7. Long ears were put on Hector rabbits.

____

8. He used soft balls for the rabbits tails.

____

Notes for Home: Your child wrote possessive forms of nouns. ***Home Activity:*** List familiar people and objects. Challenge your child to choose one word from each list and put them together, using the possessive form of one noun.

Name ________________________________

Possessive Nouns

Directions: The signs at the zoo are written incorrectly. Each one should have a possessive noun. Write the possessive form.

seals pool	alligator island	tigers house	bird cage

1. ____________________ **3.** ____________________

2. ____________________ **4.** ____________________

Directions: Rewrite each sentence. Use the possessive form of the underlined noun.

5. The <u>lion</u> roar is very loud.

____

6. People laugh at the <u>monkey</u> tricks.

____

7. Children ride on the <u>horses</u> backs.

____

8. We pet the animals in the <u>lambs</u> pen.

____

9. The lambs eat from the <u>twins</u> hands.

____

Write a Song

Write a song about zoo animals. Use possessive nouns, such as those in the phrases *bears' claws* or *a giraffe's spots*. Write on a separate sheet of paper.

Notes for Home: Your child used possessive forms of nouns. ***Home Activity:*** Make a list of possessive forms of singular (one) and plural (more than one) nouns. Have your child use a highlighting marker to mark the plural possessive nouns.

Name ______________________________

Possessive Nouns

REVIEW

Directions: Write the possessive form of the word in ( ) to complete each sentence.

______________ **1.** Each spring the (town) children have a special tradition.

______________ **2.** It happens after the (tulips) buds open.

______________ **3.** It happens after they hear the first (robin) chirp.

______________ **4.** The children, with their (parents) help, clean up the park.

______________ **5.** One group puts all the litter in the (park) trash cans.

______________ **6.** Raul and his friends scrub the (playground) swings and monkey bars.

______________ **7.** The whole Li family paints all the picnic (tables) tops and benches.

______________ **8.** At the end of the clean up, (Tina) friends are tired.

______________ **9.** (Raul) friends are hot and dirty.

______________ **10.** The parents are proud of their (children) hard work.

Directions: Use the possessive form of each noun below in a sentence. Write the sentence on the line.

Yoko people cats Charles mother

11. ____

12. ____

13. ____

14. ____

15. ____

Notes for Home: Your child identified and wrote singular and plural possessive nouns. ***Home Activity:*** Put the word "one" in front of three nouns, and the word "many" in front of three other nouns. Challenge your child to write the possessive form of the noun you name.

Name ____________________

Common and Proper Nouns

Common nouns name any person, place, or thing, but they do not tell which person, which place, or which things: **girls, city, day.**

Proper nouns name a particular person, place, or thing. Begin proper nouns with a capital letter. If the proper noun has more than one word, the first word and each important word have capital letters: **Cynthia, New York City, Monday.**

Directions: Write each noun in the correct column. Capitalize the proper nouns.

barbara	restaurant	washington, d.c.	april
author	country	england	mrs. takashima
holiday	teacher	city	saturday
dr. carrera	state	arbor day	antarctic
friend	snow	dallas	birds

Common Nouns	Proper Nouns
1. ______	11. ______
2. ______	12. ______
3. ______	13. ______
4. ______	14. ______
5. ______	15. ______
6. ______	16. ______
7. ______	17. ______
8. ______	18. ______
9. ______	19. ______
10. ______	20. ______

Notes for Home: Your child identified common and proper nouns. ***Home Activity:*** Play a word game. Name a category, such as towns. Ask your child to name a specific thing that fits in that category, such as Spring Lake.

Name ___________________________________

Common and Proper Nouns

Directions: Look at the underlined nouns in each sentence. If a noun is a common noun, write **common** on the line. If it is a proper noun, write the noun correctly on the line.

My brother greg studies puffins where they live in iceland.

1. ________________ **2.** ________________ **3.** ________________

He also studies puffins that live in the eastern united states and greenland.

4. ________________ **5.** ________________ **6.** ________________

Last tuesday, he sent me a picture of puffins swimming in the atlantic ocean.

7. ________________ **8.** ________________ **9.** ________________

You can see Greg's pictures in magazines such as *national geographic*.

10. ________________ **11.** ________________ **12.** ________________

In august, my sister julie is going to visit him for a week.

13. ________________ **14.** ________________ **15.** ________________

Write an Entry in a Birder's Notebook

What kinds of birds do you see around your home or school? Where exactly do you see them? On a separate sheet of paper, write a paragraph that names the birds in your area and where you have seen them. Be sure to include both common and proper nouns in your paragraph.

Notes for Home: Your child identified common nouns and proper nouns. ***Home Activity:*** Look in a newspaper for proper nouns. Ask your child to tell why each proper noun is capitalized.

Name ______________________________

Common and Proper Nouns

RETEACHING

Look at the pictures. Write names for the girl and the school. Choose one of these names: Franklin School, Peggy Jones.

girl  school 

______________________ ______________________

A **common noun** names any person, place, or thing but it does not tell which one. A **proper noun** names a particular person, place, or thing.

Directions: Write a proper noun for each common noun. Use the proper nouns from the box.

Chicago	Buttons	Rosa Ortiz	Sunnyside Museum

1. woman ______________________ **3.** museum ______________________

2. city ______________________ **4.** dog ______________________

Directions: Write each underlined common noun and proper noun in the correct group below.

5. Utah has many interesting places.

6. Great Salt Lake is saltier than the ocean.

7. Some large rocks look like cities.

Common Nouns

______________________ ______________________

______________________ ______________________

Proper Nouns

______________________ ______________________

Notes for Home: Your child used common and proper nouns. ***Home Activity:*** Write common and proper nouns on slips of paper and put them in a box. Challenge your child to choose a slip of paper and identify the noun as common or proper.

Name ____________________

Common and Proper Nouns

Directions: Circle each common noun. Underline each proper noun.

1. Hawaii is a very beautiful state.

2. Our plane flew over the Pacific Ocean.

3. Ann Ning likes to jog along the beach.

4. Diamond Head is a famous volcano.

5. Maui was formed by two volcanic mountains.

6. Did your friend visit Hawaii Volcanoes National Park?

Directions: Underline the nouns in the note. Then write each one in the correct group.

7.–16.

Tracy,

Hawaii has many islands. Aunt Jo lives on Oahu. Her cat is named Mr. Meow. Honolulu is the largest city. It is also the capital.

Common Nouns	Proper Nouns	
____________	____________	____________
____________	____________	____________
____________	____________	____________
____________		

Write a Paragraph

Write a paragraph about a place you would like to visit. Use common nouns and proper nouns in your sentences. Write on a separate sheet of paper.

Notes for Home: Your child identified common and proper nouns. ***Home Activity:*** Together, create a story using five common nouns and three proper nouns. Have your child write the story, using capital letters for the proper nouns.

Name ______________________________

Predicates

REVIEW

Directions: Underline the complete predicate in each sentence.

1. Every night, I get ready for bed.

2. I brush my teeth.

3. I choose my clothes for the next day.

4. Sometimes my dad reads me a story.

5. Other nights, my mom sings songs.

6. My class wrote and illustrated a book.

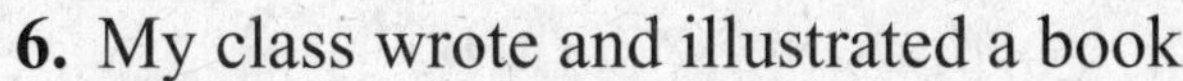

7. We painted and drew illustrations for the book.

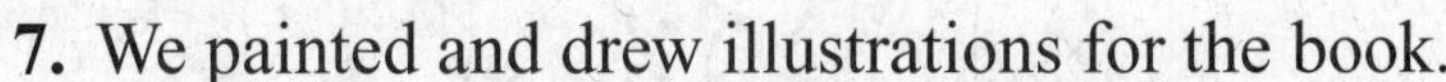

8. Our teacher read the words and typed them on the computer.

9. We edited and retyped the book.

10. We cheered and had a party when we were done.

Directions: Write a predicate to complete each sentence.

11. My mother _____.

____

12. She _____.

____

13. She and I _____.

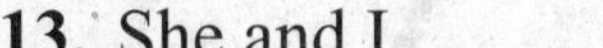

____

14. We _____.

____

15. My mother _____.

____

Notes for Home: Your child identified and wrote predicates—the part of the sentence that tells what the subject is or does. ***Home Activity:*** Write five subjects on slips of paper. Have your child draw a slip of paper and make up a predicate to go with the subject.

Name ___________________________________

Verbs

An **action verb** is a word that shows action.

Mr. Green played the piano.   Mrs. Green ate dinner.

A **linking verb** links, or joins, a subject to a word in the predicate. It does not show action. *Am, is, are, was,* and *were* are linking verbs.

The elephant is large.   Ants are small.

Directions: Write an action verb to complete each sentence.

1. Authors __________ books.

2. A baker __________ bread and cake.

3. The plumber __________ broken water pipes.

4. Ms. Mackin, the carpenter, __________ cabinets.

5. The sales clerk __________ toys.

6. Doctors __________ people feel better.

7. Letter carriers __________ mail.

8. Painters __________ beautiful pictures.

9. Mrs. Salmi __________ music in school.

10. People with different jobs __________ different things.

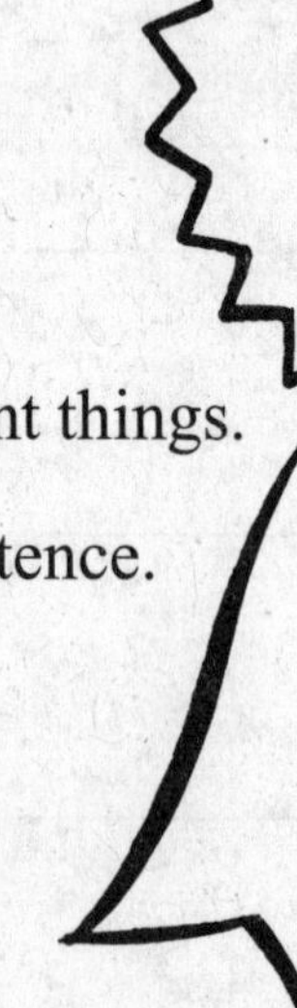

Directions: Underline the linking verb in each sentence.

11. There are twenty-seven children in my class.

12. Today, we are all happy.

13. One of us is the winner of a big contest.

14. His poem was the best of all.

15. We are all very proud of him

Notes for Home: Your child identified action and linking verbs. ***Home Activity:*** Make up silly sentences for your child and have him or her identify the verbs and tell whether each one is an action verb or a linking verb.

Name ______________________________

Verbs

Directions: Underline the verb in each sentence. Write **A** if the verb is an action verb. Write **L** if the verb is a linking verb.

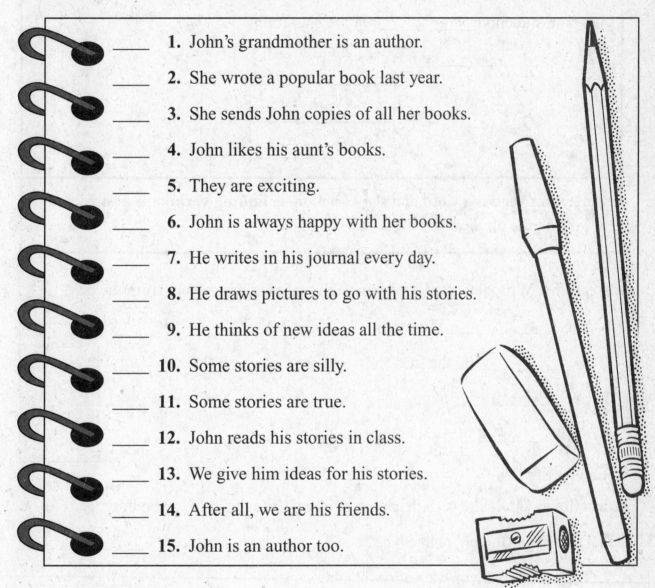

____ **1.** John's grandmother is an author.

____ **2.** She wrote a popular book last year.

____ **3.** She sends John copies of all her books.

____ **4.** John likes his aunt's books.

____ **5.** They are exciting.

____ **6.** John is always happy with her books.

____ **7.** He writes in his journal every day.

____ **8.** He draws pictures to go with his stories.

____ **9.** He thinks of new ideas all the time.

____ **10.** Some stories are silly.

____ **11.** Some stories are true.

____ **12.** John reads his stories in class.

____ **13.** We give him ideas for his stories.

____ **14.** After all, we are his friends.

____ **15.** John is an author too.

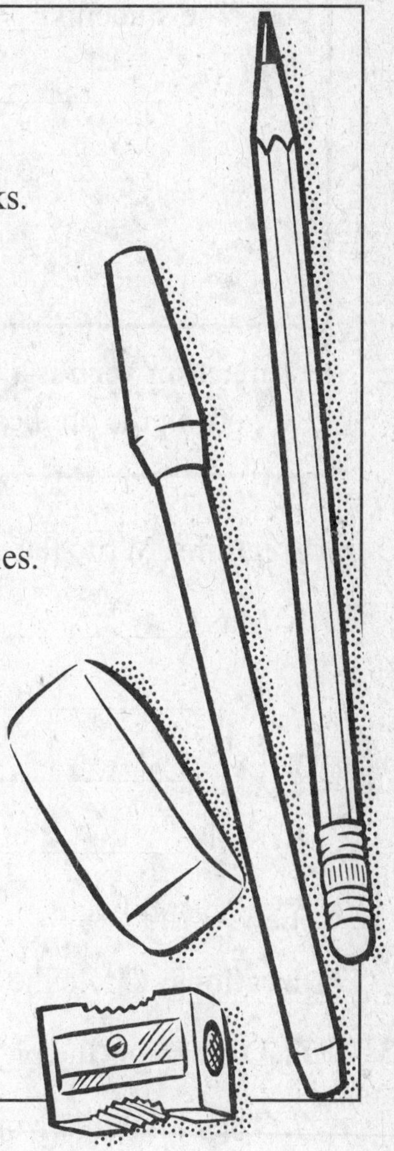

Write a Book Proposal

On a separate sheet of paper, describe a book you would like to write. Tell who is in the book and what happens to them. When you're done, go back and underline all the verbs you wrote.

Notes for Home: Your child identified action verbs and linking verbs, such as *is, are, was,* and *were*. ***Home Activity:*** Pick a letter of the alphabet and take turns with your child naming all the verbs you can think of beginning with that letter.

Verbs

RETEACHING

Complete each sentence. Use a verb from the box.

1. The students ____________ in the classroom.

2. We ____________ in our classroom.

Verbs	
read	are

An **action verb** is a word that shows action. A **linking verb** joins a subject to a word in the predicate.

Directions: Write the correct verb in each sentence. Use a verb from the box.

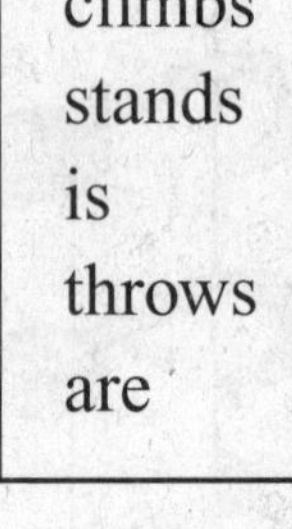

climbs
stands
is
throws
are

1. Max ____________ the ball.

2. Joe ____________ the tree.

3. Lee ____________ happy.

4. Kelly ____________ on her head.

5. Juan and Ivan ____________ on their towels.

Directions: Circle the verb in each sentence. Write the verb on the line.

6. Dara opens the big picnic basket. ____________

7. The children are on the yellow blanket. ____________

8. Joe pours the juice into paper cups. ____________

9. The children drink the cold juice. ____________

10. The fresh, cold juice is tasty. ____________

Notes for Home: Your child identified and wrote verbs in sentences. ***Home Activity:*** Write five sentences, leaving blank lines in place of verbs. Have your child think of silly verbs and fill in the blanks with those verbs.

Name ______________________________

Verbs

Directions: Discover the bird in the puzzle. First, underline the verb in each sentence. Then write the verbs in the blanks.

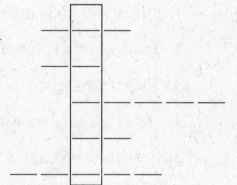

1. Birds are very busy animals.
2. They go among the branches.
3. They build nests there.
4. The mother is on her nest.
5. She sings to her baby birds.

Directions: Circle the verb in each sentence. Then write a new sentence using that verb.

6. The babies sleep in the nest.

____

7. The mother bird is on the ground.

____

8. It finds food for its babies.

____

9. The little birds open their mouths wide.

____

Write a Poem

Write a poem about a bird you have seen or read about. Use verbs to describe what you know about the bird. Use at least one linking verb and two action verbs. Write on a separate sheet of paper.

Notes for Home: Your child identified verbs in sentences. ***Home Activity:*** Have your child cut out verbs from magazines and newspapers and glue them on white or colored paper to make a verb collage.

Name ________________________________

REVIEW

Verbs

Directions: Underline the verb in each sentence. Write **A** if the verb is an action verb. Write **L** if the verb is a linking verb.

________ **1.** Keisha and Kathi are sisters.

________ **2.** They put up a booth on their lawn.

________ **3.** They sell things to their neighbors.

________ **4.** Today is a very hot day.

________ **5.** Lemonade is great for thirsty people.

________ **6.** Today Keisha and Kathi made lemonade.

________ **7.** They carefully squeezed the lemons.

________ **8.** They stirred in some sugar.

________ **9.** They added a few ice cubes.

________ **10.** They sold the lemonade to thirsty people.

Directions: Choose a verb that best completes each sentence. Write the verb on the line to the left.

________________ **11.** People _____ lots of lemonade from Keisha and Kathi.

________________ **12.** The lemonade _____ cool and not too tart.

________________ **13.** Keisha and Kathi _____ more lemonade.

________________ **14.** Soon, they _____ out of lemons.

________________ **15.** So, Kathi _____ to the store.

Notes for Home: Your child identified and used verbs in sentences. ***Home Activity:*** Say either *action* or *linking*. Have your child say a sentence with the type of verb you named (For example: *That dog ran away yesterday. That dog is very cute.*).

Name ________________________________

Verbs in Sentences

A verb is the main word in the predicate, the part of a sentence that tells what the subject is or does.

You can combine the predicates of sentences that have the same subject. Use a conjunction, a joining word such as *and* or *or,* to combine the predicates.

The farmer planted his crops. The farmer watered his crops.
The farmer planted and watered his crops.

Sometimes one verb is made up of two words. The **main verb** is the most important verb. The **helping verb** comes before it.

The farmer has planted all his crops.

Directions: The complete predicate in each sentence is underlined. Write the verb or verbs on the line.

________________ **1.** The tortoise and the hare ran a race.

________________ **2.** The hare sprinted faster than the tortoise.

________________ **3.** The hare stopped and slept.

________________ **4.** The tortoise raced to the finish line.

________________ **5.** The tortoise won the race.

Directions: Look at each underlined verb. Write **main** if it is the main verb. Write **helping** if it is the helping verb.

________________ **6.** We have made plans for tomorrow.

________________ **7.** We are going to a farm.

________________ **8.** I am looking forward to the trip.

________________ **9.** My dad has packed lunches for us.

________________ **10.** We will pick corn for dinner.

Notes for Home: Your child identified verbs, including helping verbs, in sentences. ***Home Activity:*** Using complete sentences, tell your child five things that you saw or did today. Have your child write them down. Then ask your child to circle the verbs in your sentences.

Verbs in Sentences

Directions: Circle the verb in ( ) that correctly completes each sentence. Write the verb on the line.

______________ **1.** Sarah (were helping/was helping) her dad plant seeds.

______________ **2.** They (were digging/was dug) holes in the ground.

______________ **3.** Earlier that morning, they (were decided/had decided) which seeds to plant.

______________ **4.** Now, they (were dropping and covering/has dropped and covered) the seeds.

______________ **5.** "I (am working/is working) very hard," said Sarah proudly.

Directions: Underline the complete predicate. Then put a second line under each verb. Remember that a sentence may have more than one verb. Be sure to include all helping verbs.

6. The children went to the apple orchard and played games.

7. They walked and rode their bikes.

8. In the orchard, some children ran around and played tag.

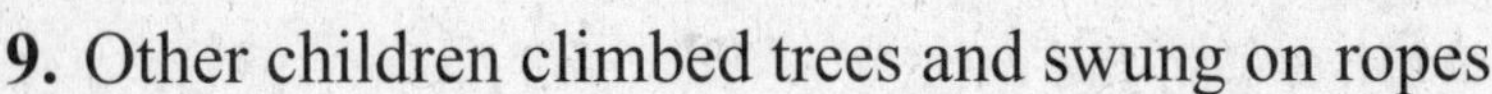

9. Other children climbed trees and swung on ropes.

10. By sunset they had played many games and were tired.

Write a Diary Entry

Some people keep a diary. In a diary, you write what you did and what you saw. On a separate sheet of paper, write a diary entry for last weekend. Be sure to use helping verbs.

Notes for Home: Your child identified verbs in sentences, including sentences with more than one verb. ***Home Activity:*** Write sentences telling your child to do two things (For example, *Please jump and sing.*). Have your child identify the verbs, then carry out the instructions.

Verbs in Sentences

RETEACHING

Write a verb or verbs to complete each sentence.

1. Three cows __________ and __________ in the meadow.

2. Some people __________ them closely.

3. They ________________ pictures.

The main word in a predicate is a **verb**. It tells what the subject is or does. When a verb is made up of two words, the main verb is the more important verb, and the helping verb comes before it.

Directions: The predicate is underlined in each sentence. Circle each verb.

1. They take paints and brushes with them.

2. They stop near the grassy meadow.

3. Four bluebirds are resting in the tall, soft grass.

4. Yellow flowers grow under their feet.

5. Some squirrels jump and play in an oak tree.

6. The women talk in soft voices.

Directions: Write a verb in the predicate of each sentence. Use a word from the box.

opens	paints	is carrying	sparkles	puts

7. Debra ________________ a cloth bag of paints.

8. She ________________ a tube of green paint.

9. She ________________ some on a long, thin brush.

10. She ________________ the gentle green meadow.

11. The wet grass ________________ in the sunlight.

Notes for Home: Your child identified and wrote verbs in sentences. ***Home Activity:*** Write verbs on slips of paper. Take turns with your child, acting out a verb and having the other person guess the verb that is being pantomimed.

Name ______________________________

Verbs in Sentences

Directions: The predicate in each sentence is underlined. Circle the verb.

1. The farmer plants rows of bushes.
2. Berries are growing on the low bushes.
3. Sun and water have helped them grow.
4. Some workers pick the ripe, juicy berries.
5. Their alarm clocks wake them at six o'clock.
6. They work in the early morning.

Directions: Complete each predicate with a verb or verbs. Use verbs from the box.

sniffs	washes	dries	drives	are loading	invites	will eat	bakes	buys

7. Workers ____________________ the berries on a truck.
8. A truck driver ____________________ them to the market.
9. Dad ____________________ several boxes there.
10. Mom __________ and __________ the berries.
11. My brother ____________________ some bread in the oven.
12. Mr. Beard ____________________ a wonderful smell.
13. Dad ____________________ him for a snack.
14. My brother ____________________ three big pieces.

Write a Funny Story

On a separate sheet of paper, write a funny story about something you have cooked or would like to cook. Be sure to use action and linking verbs.

Notes for Home: Your child identified and wrote verbs in sentences. ***Home Activity:*** Look at a magazine or newspaper article together and have your child circle the verbs with colored pencils.

Name ____________________

Verbs in Sentences

REVIEW

Directions: Circle the verb or verbs in each sentence. Remember to circle helping verbs too.

1. Felicia has wanted a pet cat for a long time.
2. Her parents will buy her one today.
3. They go to a cat breeder's house.
4. The woman has lots of beautiful cats.
5. The cats are allowed all over the house.
6. Felicia sees a calico kitten.
7. She sighs and points to it.
8. Her parents would like the tiger-striped cat.
9. However, they buy Felicia the calico kitten instead.
10. The new kitten's name is Sneakers.

Directions: Circle the verb in ( ) that correctly completes each sentence. Write the verb on the line.

________ **11.** Tommy (will love/loved) his new dog from the moment he got him.

________ **12.** Yesterday he (will name/named) the dog Rufus.

________ **13.** Now Rufus and Tommy (jogged/are jogging) in the park.

________ **14.** When Rufus sees a squirrel, he (chases/had chased) it.

________ **15.** Next time, Tommy (was keeping/will keep) Rufus on a leash.

Notes for Home: Your child identified verbs in sentences. ***Home Activity:*** Play "Animal Action" with your child. Take turns naming different kinds of animals and giving verbs that go with each animal. *(Fish swim. Birds chirp.)*

Name ______________________________

Verb Tenses: Present, Past, and Future

A verb in the **present tense** shows action that is happening now. Many verbs in the present tense end with **-s** or **-es.**

A verb in the **past tense** shows action that has already happened. Many verbs in the past tense end with **-ed.** Sometimes you have to change the spelling before adding **-ed.** Some past tense verbs do not use **-ed** endings.

A verb in the **future tense** shows action that will happen. Verbs in the future tense use the helping verb *will.*

Verb	Present Tense	Past Tense	Future Tense
play	He plays.	She played.	We will play.
try	She tries.	They tried.	I will try.
take	She takes.	I took.	She will take.

Directions: Circle the verb in each sentence. If there is a helping verb and main verb, circle both. Then write **present, past,** or **future** on the line to show the tense.

______________ **1.** Yesterday, Margie lost her baseball.

______________ **2.** She tried to find it until sundown.

______________ **3.** "We will look for it tomorrow."

______________ **4.** Their dog Poncho always finds things.

______________ **5.** He will find the ball.

______________ **6.** That night, Poncho brought the ball to Margie.

______________ **7.** Margie hugged Poncho as hard as she could.

______________ **8.** Margie threw the ball very far.

______________ **9.** Poncho brings the ball back to her.

______________ **10.** "Tomorrow we will play again, Poncho."

Notes for Home: Your child identified verbs in the past tense, present tense, and future tense. ***Home Activity:*** Read a favorite book with your child. Challenge your child to identify the tenses of some of the verbs. Ask your child to rewrite the verbs in each of the other two tenses.

Name ______________________________________

Verb Tenses: Present, Past, and Future

Directions: Underline the verb in each sentence. Remember to include helping verbs. Then circle a word in ( ) to tell the tense of each verb.

1. Tomorrow, we will get a new dog.
(past/present/future)

2. We waited for weeks.
(past/present/future)

3. Yesterday, we bought some food and toys.
(past/present/future)

4. Today, we are looking for a dog bed.
(past/present/future)

5. We will have fun with our new best friend.
(past/present/future)

Directions: Choose a verb in the tense shown in ( ) to complete each sentence. Write the verb on the line to the left.

________________ **6.** The police officer __________ a dog to our school. (past)

________________ **7.** The dog __________ how she helps the police. (past)

________________ **8.** The police officer __________ the dog to work tomorrow. (future)

________________ **9.** The dog __________ at our school. (present)

________________ **10.** The students __________ the police dog. (present)

Write an Activities List

What do you like to do with your friends? Did you do the same things when you were younger? Or did you do different things back then? On a separate sheet of paper, write about things that you like to do with friends. Include things you did when you were younger and things you want to do when you are older. Use different tenses.

Notes for Home: Your child identified and wrote verbs to show events that happened in the past, present, and future. ***Home Activity:*** Ask your child to name some favorite songs. Ask your child to sing a line or two and then identify the verb tenses.

Name ______________________________

RETEACHING

Verb Tenses: Present, Past, and Future

Read the sentence. It uses a verb in the present tense.

1. We paint the house.

Write the sentence. Make it tell about a time in the past. Add **-ed** to the verb.

2. ______________________________

Now write the sentence so it tells about action in the future. Use the helping verb **will.**

3. ______________________________

A verb in the **present tense** shows action that happens now. When a noun is singular, a verb in the present tense ends in **-s** or **-es**. A verb in the **past tense** shows action that already happened. Most verbs in the past tense end in **-ed.** A verb in the **future tense** shows action that will happen in the future. Verbs in the future tense have the helping verb **will** followed by the main verb.

Directions: The verb is underlined in each sentence. Write each past-tense verb on the line to the right.

1. My friend Gary <u>helped</u> me with it. ____________

2. We <u>hammered</u> nails along the edges. ____________

3. Max <u>sits</u> proudly in his new house. ____________

Directions: Fill in each blank with the correct form of the verb in ( ).

4. Tina ____________ the weeds in the garden soon. (pick)

5. She ____________ the plants along the fence yesterday. (water)

6. Tomorrow they ____________ the potatoes and carrots. (peel)

Notes for Home: Your child identified and used verbs in different tenses. ***Home Activity:*** Write a letter to your child. Read it together and have your child point out all the verbs written in the present tense.

Name ______________________________

Verb Tenses: Present, Past, and Future

Directions: Complete each sentence. Write the correct verb from the camera.

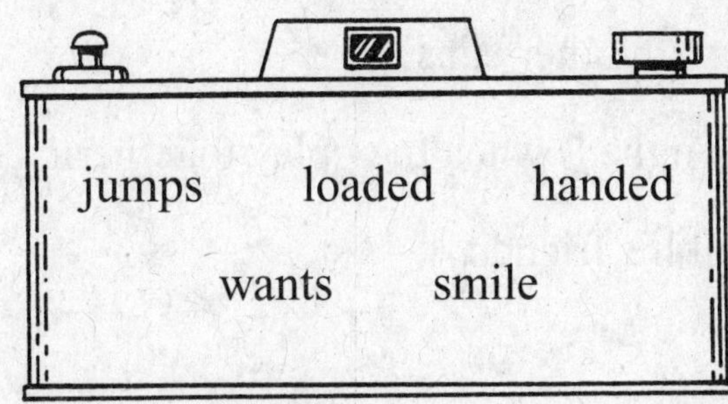

1. David's uncle ______________ him a new camera.
2. Then David ______________ it with film.
3. Three friends ______________ for a picture now.
4. Frisky ______________ onto Pat's lap.
5. The puppy ______________ to be in the picture too.

Directions: Complete each sentence. Write the correct verb in ( ).

6. Then they ______________ at the puppy. (laugh/laughed/will laugh)
7. When it is time to take the picture, they ______________ into the camera. (stare/stared/will stare)
8. Now the new camera ______________ softly. (clicks/clicked/will click)
9. When he heard the sound, Frisky ______________ under the sofa. (runs/ran/will run)

Write a Description

Describe things you can do now that you couldn't do when you were younger. Use verbs in the correct tenses. Write on a separate sheet of paper.

Notes for Home: Your child used verbs in the present, past, and future tenses. ***Home Activity:*** Read a story with your child. Have him or her list verbs in the past tense. Challenge your child to list the same verbs in the present and future tenses.

Name ______________________________

Using Verb Tenses Correctly

REVIEW

Directions: Circle the verb in the present tense to complete each sentence.

1. The bear cub (lived/lives) in a den in the forest.

2. He (will play/plays) with other cubs.

3. All the cubs (laugh/laughed) when they play together.

4. He (likes/will like) all his friends.

Directions: Circle the verb in the past tense to complete each sentence.

5. His mother (looks/looked) at picture books with the bear cub.

6. One of the books (scares/scared) him.

7. His mother (hugged/hugs) him.

8. Then he (brushes/brushed) his teeth and went to bed.

Directions: Circle the verb in the future tense to complete each sentence.

9. When he grows up, the cub (looks/will look) at picture books with his children.

10. He (will hug/hugged) them every night.

Directions: Rewrite each sentence using the correct verb tense.

11. Yesterday, I travel to the zoo. ______________________________

12. Tomorrow, I walk to the library. ______________________________

13. Now my dad hugged me. ______________________________

14. I visit Sandy last week. ______________________________

15. Next summer, I lived at the beach. ______________________________

Notes for Home: Your child identified and used different verb tenses to show something happening in the past, present, or future. ***Home Activity:*** Take turns telling a story with your child. Start in the past, move to the present, and end in the future.

Forms of Regular Verbs

When you write, you use different forms of a verb for different tenses.

I walk. She will walk. We are walking. They walked.

Here are some verbs that have similar forms. They are called **regular verbs.** They are shown with sample subjects.

The verb	The –s form	The –ing form	The –ed form
We jump.	Sam jumps.	Lisa is jumping.	A frog jumped.
I will live.	She lives.	They were living.	A plant lived.
You watch.	Chiyo watches.	We are watching.	Ricky watched.

Directions: Circle the correct form of the verb in ( ) to complete each sentence. Write the verb on the line.

______________ **1.** Today our class will (presenting/present) a play.

______________ **2.** We are (pretending/pretends) we are aliens from Venus.

______________ **3.** When we practiced the play, Ellen (appeared/appear) in a purple costume.

______________ **4.** She (looking/looked) like a purple grape, not an alien.

______________ **5.** Ellen felt as if she had (embarrass/embarrassed) herself.

______________ **6.** Ellen and her father (added/adding) antennas and wings to her costume.

______________ **7.** They were (changing/changed) the grape into a funny alien.

Directions: Draw a line from the sentence on the left to the correct verb form on the right to complete each sentence.

8. Ellen and I _____ in a play last year. **a.** act

9. We like to _____ in funny scenes. **b.** acting

10. This year Ellen is _____ as an alien. **c.** acted

Notes for Home: Your child learned about forms of regular verbs (For example: *look, looks, is looking, looked*). ***Home Activity:*** Ask your child to make up sentences that use different forms of these verbs: *jump (jumps, jumping, jumped)* and *walk (walks, walking, walked)*.

Name ____________________

Forms of Regular Verbs

Directions: Circle the correct form of the verb in ( ) to complete each sentence. Write the verb on the line.

______________ **1.** I (perform/performing) in the school talent show every year.

______________ **2.** Tonight, I will (dances/dance) in the opening number.

______________ **3.** My sister always (helps/helping) me with my dance steps.

______________ **4.** My friend Maria is (dances/dancing) with me.

______________ **5.** We (like/likes) to make up dances to our favorite songs.

______________ **6.** We (practice/practices) in Maria's basement.

______________ **7.** The whole school is (looks/looking) at us as we perform.

______________ **8.** When the music (start/starts), I no longer feel nervous.

______________ **9.** I (waits/waited) all year for this night.

Directions: Use the correct form of the verb in ( ) to complete each sentence. Write the verb on the line.

______________ **10.** Last night we (walk) onto the stage and the crowd cheered.

______________ **11.** Tonight, Maria (walk) right beside me.

______________ **12.** She is (walk) to the center of the stage.

______________ **13.** After we danced, we (watch) the other performers.

______________ **14.** We are (watch) from behind the curtain.

______________ **15.** Everyone always (watch) the jugglers very carefully.

Write a Letter

On a separate sheet of paper, write a letter telling a friend about a time you were afraid to try something new. Use different verb forms for different tenses.

Notes for Home: Your child used different forms of a verb for different tenses (For example: *I am dancing. She danced.*). ***Home Activity:*** Write some action verbs such as *dance* or *hop* on slips of paper. Have your child act out each verb and say the verb in its different forms.

Name ________________________________

RETEACHING

Forms of Regular Verbs

Noun	Present-Tense Verb	Past-Tense Verb
girl	plays	played
girls	play	played
painter	paints	painted
painters	paint	painted
mover	packs	packed
movers	pack	packed

Complete each sentence. Write a noun and a verb from the box above.

1. One ____________________ ____________________ in the park.
2. Some ____________________ ____________________ the dishes.

A verb in the present tense shows action that happens now. Add **-s** or **-es** to the verb when the noun is singular. A verb in the past tense shows action that happened in the past. Add **-ed** to the verb.

Directions: Circle a verb in ( ) that makes sense in the sentence.

1. Movers (lifts/lifted) heavy boxes off the truck when the family arrived.
2. Mr. Owen (fix/fixes) the kitchen cabinets.
3. The children (wave/waves) across the street.
4. Now the painters (paint/paints) the house.
5. Mrs. Owen (want/wanted) bright colors.
6. The children (watch/watches) the painters.
7. One of them (clean/cleaned) his paintbrushes after he used them.
8. The painters (finished/finishes) two rooms in one day.

Notes for Home: Your child identified forms of regular verbs—verbs that use an *-ed* ending in the past tense. ***Home Activity:*** Have your child draw himself or herself playing. Encourage your child to write sentences about the picture, using regular verbs.

Name ___________________________

Forms of Regular Verbs

Directions: Complete each sentence with a verb from the box. The word in ( ) tells you which verb tense to use.

travel	talk	explore	cover	pull

1. Mrs. Cruz _______________ about Richard Byrd. (present)

2. He _______________ to Antarctica. (past)

3. A sheet of ice _______________ most of the land. (present)

4. A team of dogs _______________ sleds over the ice. (past)

5. Richard Byrd _______________ the land there. (past)

Directions: Write the verb in ( ) in the past tense. Write one letter on each line. Then use the circled letters to answer the question below.

6. The unusual birds (shock) him. ___ ___ ___ (___) ___ ___ ___

7. He (enjoy) the playful birds. ___ ___ ___ (___) ___ ___ ___

8. They (walk) quickly on the ice. ___ ___ (___) ___ ___ ___

9. The black and white feathers (look) like a suit. ___ ___ ___ ___ ___ (___)

How does it feel in Antarctica? ___ ___ ___ ___

Write an Adventure Story

Imagine going on an adventure to somewhere you have never been. You may only take with you what you can carry in a backpack. On a separate sheet of paper, write a story about your adventure. Use correct verb forms in your sentences.

Notes for Home: Your child used regular verbs in sentences. ***Home Activity:*** Tell a story to your child. Challenge your child to listen to the story and write a list of regular verbs used in the story.

Name ______________________________

Forms of Regular Verbs

REVIEW

Directions: Circle the verb in ( ) that best completes each sentence.

1. My dad has (living/lived) in this neighborhood his whole life.

2. He (played/plays) on this playground when he was a boy.

3. He (will attend/attended) this school when he was young.

4. We still (living/live) in the house where he grew up.

5. Today he (talking/talks) about what it was like back then.

6. Back then my dad (walked/walking) a mile to school.

7. Today I go to the same school, but my brother and I (taking/take) the bus.

8. When my dad was my age, he (practices/practiced) basketball after school.

9. I (liked/like) to ride my skateboard when I play after school.

10. When my dad had time, he (helps/helped) his parents in their store.

11. I (ask/asked) my dad if I could help him at work, but he said I was too young.

12. When I turn 14, I will (working/work) with him in his office.

Directions: Draw a line from the sentence on the left to the correct verb form on the right to finish each sentence.

13. Every time my dad talks about growing up, he _____ a lot.	**a.** laughs
14. When he told the story about his two goofy dogs, I _____.	**b.** laughing
15. My dad and I are always_____ when he tells his old stories.	**c.** laughed

Notes for Home: Your child has learned about the forms of regular verbs. ***Home Activity:*** Name some regular verbs (verbs that use an *-ed* ending in past tense, such as *play, jump,* and *learn*) on cards. Have your child name the different verb forms (endings with *-s,* with *-ing,* and with *-ed.*).

Name ____________________

Forms of Irregular Verbs

Verbs that do not add **-ed** to show past action are called **irregular verbs**. Because irregular verbs do not follow a regular pattern, you must remember their spellings.

The Verb	The –s Form	The –ing Form	The Past Form
run	runs	running	ran
begin	begins	beginning	began
take	takes	taking	took
go	goes	going	went

Directions: Circle the correct form of the irregular verb in ( ) to complete each sentence. Write the verb on the line.

__________ **1.** Molly is (ran/running) in a road race tomorrow.

__________ **2.** She (run/runs) every day after school.

__________ **3.** Her father (ran/runs) when he was in school too.

__________ **4.** He is (go/going) to run with Molly in the race.

__________ **5.** Molly's dad (takes/took) her to watch a marathon last year.

__________ **6.** The race (beginning/began) in their town and ended in the city.

__________ **7.** They (went/goes) into the city to see the finish line.

__________ **8.** Molly (seeing/saw) the winner cross the finish line.

__________ **9.** Molly's dad was (take/taking) pictures as the winner crossed.

__________ **10.** She (thought/think) she would like to win the marathon someday.

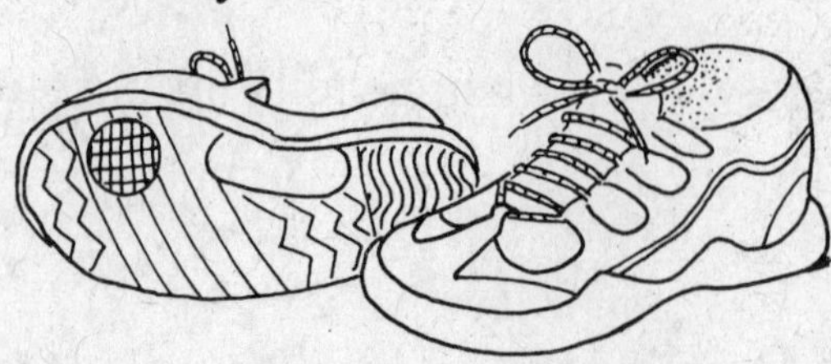

Notes for Home: Your child used different forms of irregular verbs—verbs that don't take *-ed* to form the past tense. ***Home Activity:*** Challenge your child to name as many irregular verbs as he or she can. Work with your child to write the past tense of each verb.

Name ____________________

Forms of Irregular Verbs

Directions: Use the correct form of the irregular verb in ( ) to complete each sentence. Write the verb on the line.

__________ **1.** Last year, my dad and I (go) to the town where he grew up.

__________ **2.** We (see) the house where he used to live.

__________ **3.** He (buy) me a cap at his favorite sports store.

__________ **4.** Dad said he (know) the man who owned the store.

__________ **5.** I'm so glad Dad (take) me with him!

Directions: Rewrite each sentence in the past tense on the line. Be sure to use the correct verb forms.

6. My dad does some cool things! __________

7. My dad swims at the town pool. __________

8. He dives off the diving board too. __________

9. He runs in school races. __________

10. My dad is so much like me. __________

Write a Comparison

On a separate sheet of paper, compare how you and an older family member are alike and different. Ask older family members what they liked to do when they were your age. Try to include different forms of some irregular verbs.

Notes for Home: Your child wrote different forms of irregular verbs (verbs that don't end with *-ed* in the past tense; for example: *bought* and *sold*). ***Home Activity:*** Make flash cards with irregular verbs *(take, swim, buy, think, know)*. Ask your child to say the verb's past tense form.

Name ____________________

Forms of Irregular Verbs

RETEACHING

Verb	do	go	eat	give	see
Past	did	went	ate	gave	saw
Past with <u>have</u>, <u>has</u>, or <u>had</u>	done	gone	eaten	given	seen

Read each sentence. Then circle the past-tense form of the verb **go** or **see.**

1. They went to the fair. **2.** They saw many happy people.

Regular verbs that show the past end in **-ed. Irregular verbs** change their forms to show the past.

Directions: Write the correct past-tense form of each underlined verb.

1. Then they <u>do</u> something funny. ____________

2. They <u>go</u> to the Fun House of Mirrors. ____________

3. The mirrors <u>give</u> them quite a surprise. ____________

4. They <u>see</u> two tall and very thin people. ____________

Directions: Underline the correct form of the verb in ( ).

5. She had (saw/seen) a shiny red car.

6. She (gave/given) the wheel a sharp turn.

7. Crash! She (done/did) it!

8. Tina had (gone/went) into the next car.

9. The car had (done/did) no harm.

Notes for Home: Your child identified forms of irregular verbs. ***Home Activity:*** Write *go, goes, went, do, does, did, is, was,* and *were* on slips of paper. Have your child organize them by verb *(go, goes, went)* or by tense *(went, did, was).*

Name ___________________________

Forms of Irregular Verbs

Directions: Help proofread the report. Rewrite each verb, using the past-tense form of the underlined verb. Remember that the past-tense forms of some verbs do not end in **-ed**. Here are some examples of irregular verbs:

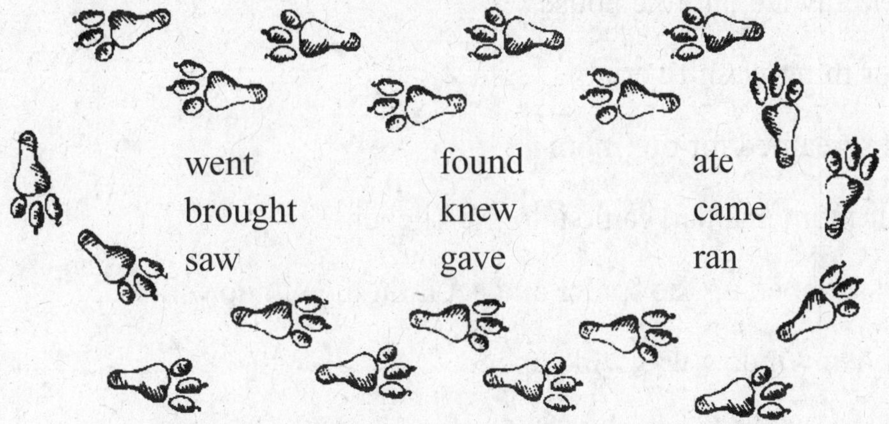

went	found	ate
brought	knew	came
saw	gave	ran

LATEST PET FAD HITS TOWN

Mr. P. Lee <u>finds</u> an odd creature yesterday. The surprised man <u>gives</u> it food. The large pink Floopit <u>eats</u> candy from his hand.

Ms. Q. Pratt <u>sees</u> a green-and-white-checked critter in her yard. The frightened woman <u>runs</u> away. This odd Checkzeet <u>comes</u> when called by name. Isn't it amazing that this big-beaked creature <u>knows</u> its name?

Notes for Home: Your child changed irregular verbs (verbs that do not take *-ed* in the past tense) to their past forms. ***Home Activity:*** Look at a magazine article together and challenge your child to rewrite the irregular verbs in the past tense.

Complete Subjects

REVIEW

Directions: Underline the complete subject in each sentence.

1. My older sister Monica is afraid of spiders.
2. A spider crawled into the house.
3. The poor thing wasn't very big.
4. Monica screamed for our mom.
5. Both our mom and dad came into the kitchen.
6. Our dad scooped up the spider and set it on the windowsill.
7. The kitchen window was wide open.
8. The frightened spider crawled right out.
9. My silly sister Monica felt much better.
10. Monica and I could now eat breakfast in peace.

Directions: Add a complete subject to finish each sentence. Remember, good subjects can be long or short. Write the subject on the line.

11. ____________________ saw a big, black spider in the barn.
12. ____________________ was spinning a web in the corner.
13. ____________________ had a beautiful pattern.
14. ____________________ was stuck in the web.
15. ____________________ ate the fly.

Notes for Home: Your child identified complete subjects. ***Home Activity:*** Ask your child to identify the complete subject in sentences.

Name ______________________________

Adjectives

An **adjective** is a word that can tell more about a noun. Adjectives can tell you how a person, place, or thing looks, tastes, sounds, or smells. Adjectives can also tell you how much or how many.

I ate <u>many</u> <u>red</u> strawberries.

A, an, and *the* are called **articles.** Articles go before nouns and sometimes before adjectives that describe.

I ate <u>an</u> apple. I ate <u>a</u> ripe banana.
I was too full to eat <u>the</u> sweet cherries.

Directions: Underline the adjective or adjectives in each sentence. Underline any articles too.

1. Kwame and Diane made a huge, icy smoothie for dessert.
2. They filled the blender with two cups of ripe raspberries and one cup of fresh strawberries.
3. Then, Kwame added a cup of cold juice.
4. They put in three cups of chopped ice and blended the delicious mixture.
5. It was a healthful dessert!

Directions: Add an adjective to make each sentence more interesting. Write the adjective on the line to the left.

______________ **6.** We had a _____ family meal last night.

______________ **7.** I set the plates of food on our _____ kitchen table.

______________ **8.** One platter was piled high with _____ sandwiches.

______________ **9.** The other platter was filled with _____ vegetables.

______________ **10.** _____ glasses were filled with homemade lemonade.

______________ **11.** There was plenty of _____ food for everyone.

Notes for Home: Your child identified and chose adjectives—words that can tell about nouns—in sentences. Your child also identified the articles *a, an,* and *the*. ***Home Activity:*** Ask your child to describe a family meal using adjectives to describe the different things on the table.

Name ___________________________________

Adjectives

Directions: Choose the adjective or article from the box that best completes each sentence. Write the word on the line to the left. Each word will be used once.

a	an	bright	crunchy	different	juicy	long	one	the	two

_______________ **1.** We decided to plan _____ potluck picnic.

_______________ **2.** On the chalkboard, we listed many _____ foods.

_______________ **3.** Then, everyone picked _____ thing to bring.

_______________ **4.** We sent out invitations to all _____ guests.

_______________ **5.** It was cloudy when the picnic started, but soon the _____ yellow sun was shining.

_______________ **6.** We had to wait a _____ time to eat because we let our guests get their food first.

_______________ **7.** They filled their plates with salads, steaming hamburgers, and _____ chips.

_______________ **8.** I was so hungry I took _____ hamburgers.

_______________ **9.** I ate so much I didn't have any room for the _____ watermelon I had brought to the picnic.

_______________ **10.** The picnic was such _____ amazing success that we'll probably have one again next year.

Write a Descriptive Paragraph

On a separate sheet of paper, write about a time you planned something really fun. Use adjectives to make your description interesting. Underline each adjective and article when you are done.

Notes for Home: Your child used adjectives (words that can describe nouns) and articles *(a, an,* and *the*) in sentences. ***Home Activity:*** Write different adjectives (For example: *cold, big,* and *green*) on slips of paper. Ask your child to choose an adjective and use it in a sentence.

Name ______________________________________

Adjectives

The words below may be used with nouns. Circle the words that best describe **snow**, **ball**, **lemon**, **lion**, and **fire**.

rusty

white

salty

sour

smoky

fresh

hard

flat

loud

quiet

A word that describes a person, place, or thing is an **adjective**. An adjective may tell how something looks, feels, tastes, smells, or sounds.

Directions: A noun is underlined in each sentence. Circle the adjective that tells more about the person, place, or thing the noun names.

1. A girl walked along the quiet beach.
2. The soft sand tickled her feet.
3. She sniffed the fresh air.
4. A pail lay on the clean beach.
5. Noisy crowds play in the shade.

Directions: Complete each sentence with an adjective.

6. He fills a pail with ________________ shells.
7. ________________ flowers grow on the hill.
8. ________________ sunshine fills the day.
9. She bites the ________________ peach.
10. Fish swim in the ________________ water.

Notes for Home: Your child identified and wrote adjectives in sentences. ***Home Activity:*** Have your child close his or her eyes and tell about a favorite place or event, using adjectives to describe sights, sounds, and smells.

Name ______________________________

Adjectives

Directions: Write in each sentence an adjective from the box. The sentence must make sense. Use each adjective once.

fancy	white	long	soft	wonderful	large

1. Some ______________________ webs brushed my face.
2. I looked inside a ______________________ trunk.
3. The trunk was filled with ______________________ clothes.
4. I discovered a ______________________ cape.
5. I also found a ______________________ dress.
6. I had a ______________________ morning in the attic.

Directions: Complete each sentence by adding an adjective.

7. It was a ______________________ day.
8. I explored our ______________________ attic.
9. I climbed the ______________________ stairs.
10. I opened the ______________________ door.
11. The room was filled with ______________________ furniture.
12. A ______________________ moth flew by.

Write a List

On a separate sheet of paper, list things you might find in an attic. Use an adjective to describe each one.

Notes for Home: Your child wrote adjectives in sentences. ***Home Activity:*** Together, choose an object in your home and challenge your child to describe it, using at least two adjectives.

Name ______________________________

REVIEW

Adjectives

Directions: Underline the adjective or adjectives in each sentence. Underline any articles too.

1. Celebrating the New Year in Chinatown is a fun time for me.
2. We always go to the city to watch the big, colorful parade.
3. The city is enormous.
4. Sometimes we go to the top of a tall building to see the many different sights.
5. Then we walk through the crowded streets.
6. The streets are filled with people in beautiful costumes.
7. There are loud, popping firecrackers everywhere you turn.
8. The air is filled with dusty, gray smoke.
9. My grandparents always give me sweet, golden candies.
10. When we return home, we have a delicious dinner.

Directions: Add adjectives to make each sentence more interesting. Write the new sentence on the line.

11. Dragons dance through the streets.

____

12. They have scales and tails.

____

13. Sometimes the dragons throw candy to the crowd.

____

14. Everyone crowds around the festival lions and clowns.

____

15. We always eat buns and tarts.

____

Notes for Home: Your child identified adjectives—words that can describe nouns—and used adjectives in sentences. ***Home Activity:*** Ask your child to describe a favorite holiday using adjectives to make the description more interesting.

Comparative and Superlative Adjectives

Some adjectives make comparisons. To compare two people, places, or things, you usually add **-er** to an adjective. To compare three or more nouns, you usually add **-est.**

Adjective	Comparative Form	Superlative Form
loud	louder	loudest
high	higher	highest
young	younger	youngest

Directions: Use an adjective from the table above to complete each sentence. Write the adjective on the line to the left.

____________ **1.** On Chinese New Year's Eve the fireworks started pretty loud, but then they got even _____.

____________ **2.** One firework burst even _____ than the tallest building.

____________ **3.** The last explosion noise was the _____ of them all.

____________ **4.** My little sister Min got scared because she is _____ than I.

____________ **5.** In fact, Min is the _____ person in my whole family.

Directions: Circle the correct form of the adjective in ( ) to complete each sentence.

6. Even the very (smaller/smallest) noise makes Min jump.

7. I am definitely (braver/bravest) than she is.

8. I was happy because I got to stay up (latest/later) than Min.

9. New Year's Eve was the (later/latest) I've ever stayed up.

10. I saw the (cooler/coolest) stuff I've ever seen in my whole life!

Notes for Home: Your child chose adjectives that compare people, places, and things. ***Home Activity:*** Ask your child to compare two or more objects, using words to compare (for example *smaller, smallest; bigger, biggest*).

Name ____________________________________

Comparative and Superlative Adjectives

Directions: Complete each sentence by adding **-er** or **-est** to the adjective in ( ). Write the new adjective on the line.

__________________ **1.** For the parade, Ken made the (large) dragon costume anyone had ever seen.

__________________ **2.** It was (tall) than six feet.

__________________ **3.** It even measured (long) than Sarah's snake costume.

__________________ **4.** Ken's costume was the (bright) in the whole class.

__________________ **5.** Ken was the (proud) person in the parade.

Directions: Circle the correct form of the adjective in ( ) to complete each sentence.

6. This New Year's parade lasted (longer/longest) than last year's parade.

7. It had the (larger/largest) crowd in the history of the parade.

8. There were a lot of people, even though our town is very (small/smallest).

9. The drums were the (louder/loudest) instruments in the marching band.

10. I think they were even (louder/loudest) than the fireworks that night!

Write an Advertisement

Write an advertisement for your favorite holiday or special event. Compare it to other holidays or events. Be sure to use adjectives that compare. Circle the adjectives.

Notes for Home: Your child identified adjectives that compare people, places and things. ***Home Activity***: Give your child a list of adjectives such as *quick, young,* and *old.* Ask him or her to use each of the adjectives in sentences that compare.

Name ______________________________

RETEACHING

Comparative and Superlative Adjectives

Study the picture. Then complete each sentence.

1. ____________ is stronger than Malcomb.
2. ____________ is the strongest of all.

The word **stronger** compares two people.
The word **strongest** compares three people.

One way adjectives tell more about nouns is by comparing. Use the **-er** form of an adjective to compare two persons, places, or things. Use the **-est** form to compare three or more persons, places, or things.

Directions: Write the **-er** and **-est** forms of each adjective.

1. warm ____________ ____________
2. sharp ____________ ____________
3. quick ____________ ____________
4. great ____________ ____________

Directions: Circle each correct adjective in ( ). Then write it on the line.

5. A lake is ____________ than a pond. (wider/widest)
6. She is the ____________ runner of all. (faster/fastest)
7. It is the ____________ day of the year. (colder/coldest)
8. He is the ____________ boy in class. (older/oldest)

Notes for Home: Your child identified and used comparative and superlative adjectives in sentences. ***Home Activity:*** Have your child name three animals and compare the animals using adjectives that compare. (For example: *long tail, longer tail, longest tail*)

Name ______________________________

Comparative and Superlative Adjectives

Directions: Look at the pictures. Write sentences that compare the objects, animals, or people. Use one of the adjectives next to each set of pictures. Remember to add **-er** to most adjectives when comparing two things. Add **-est** to most adjectives when comparing three or more things.

bright brighter brightest

1. ______________________________

2. ______________________________

3. ______________________________

tall taller tallest

4. ______________________________

5. ______________________________

6. ______________________________

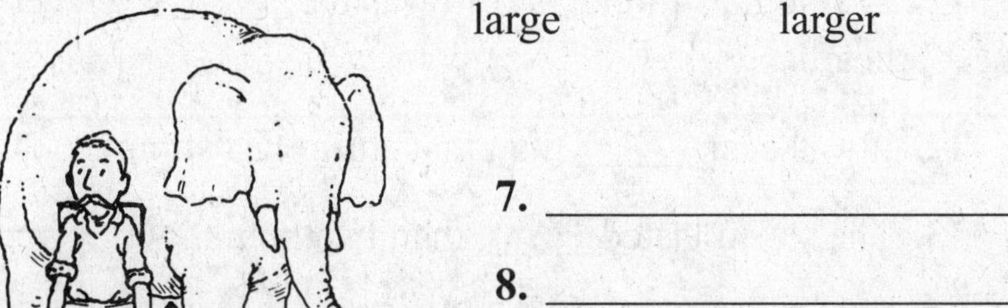

large larger largest

7. ______________________________

8. ______________________________

9. ______________________________

Notes for Home: Your child used comparative and superlative adjectives to compare objects, animals, and people. ***Home Activity:*** Find pictures of plants in magazines or books, and have your child use comparative and superlative adjectives to describe the plants.

Name ___________________________________

REVIEW

Comparative and Superlative Adjectives

Directions: Add **-er** or **-est** to the adjective in ( ) to complete each sentence. Write the new adjective on the line.

____________________ **1.** The weather was (cold) today than yesterday.

____________________ **2.** The wind grew even (strong) and more fierce.

____________________ **3.** The (tall) tree in the whole forest fell down.

____________________ **4.** It was the (loud) crash I had ever heard.

____________________ **5.** The snow was the (white) snow I had ever seen.

____________________ **6.** The (high) of the two snowdrifts reached the window.

____________________ **7.** I put on my blue coat because it was (warm) than my red one.

____________________ **8.** I pulled on the (thick) mittens I could find.

____________________ **9.** I rolled a (big) snowball than Bobby.

____________________ **10.** Billy's snowball was the (round) of the three.

Directions: Complete each sentence with a comparative or superlative adjective. Write the adjective on the line.

____________________ **11.** Last night's thunderstorm was the _____ I've ever heard.

____________________ **12.** It was even _____ than that storm last summer.

____________________ **13.** The storm lasted _____ than two hours.

____________________ **14.** I needed our _____ umbrella to go outside.

____________________ **15.** It is _____ than my brother and me put together!

Notes for Home: Your child used comparative and superlative adjectives. ***Home Activity:*** Name two or more items that have something in common. Challenge your child to compare each pair or group of items using a comparative or a superlative adjective.

Adverbs

An **adverb** is a word that can describe a verb. An adverb tells when, where, or how an action happens. Most adverbs that tell how end in **-ly.**

Carefully break the eggs. Add the vanilla later.

Adverbs can also be used to compare actions. To compare two actions, you add **-er** to many adverbs. To compare three or more actions, you add **-est.** For most adverbs that end in **-ly,** use **more** or **most** instead of **-er** and **-est.**

My cake cooked faster than his. His cake cooked more slowly.

Directions: Underline the adverb in each sentence. Use the question in ( ) to help find the adverb.

1. You can easily bake a cake yourself. (How?)
2. An adult can help you complete the job safely. (How?)
3. Cake mixes are sold everywhere. (Where?)
4. You need to wait patiently while the cake bakes. (How?)
5. If the cake is good, you can make the same kind of cake again. (When?)

Directions: Circle the correct form of the adverb in ( ) to complete each sentence. Write the adverb on the line.

____________________ **6.** The third graders finished making pizzas (quickly/more quickly) than the fourth graders.

____________________ **7.** The pepper and onion pizza cooked (fastest/faster) than the pineapple pizza.

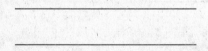

____________________ **8.** The plain pizza cooked the (faster/fastest) of all.

____________________ **9.** The whole wheat dough rose (highest/higher) than the white dough.

____________________ **10.** The teachers waited to see which of the two classes would clean up (carefully/more carefully).

Notes for Home: Your child identified adverbs—words that modify verbs telling when, where, or how an action happens. ***Home Activity:*** Have your child help you prepare dinner. Then ask him or her to describe the process using as many adverbs as possible.

Name ______________________________

Adverbs

Directions: Circle all the adverbs in the box. Then write each adverb on a line.

again	beautiful	big	easily	far	fly	girl
happily	later	perfectly	plane	pretty	quickly	red
sadly	soon	swim	tomorrow	talk	tight	tall

1. ______________________ **6.** ______________________

2. ______________________ **7.** ______________________

3. ______________________ **8.** ______________________

4. ______________________ **9.** ______________________

5. ______________________ **10.** ______________________

Directions: Use the form of the adverb in ( ) that best completes each sentence. Write the adverb on the line.

______________ **11.** I was the (careful) of all when I cracked the eggs in my cake mix.

______________ **12.** Then I stirred the batter even (fast) than the electric mixer.

______________ **13.** My cake baked (slow) than I thought it would.

______________ **14.** Tonight, my family and I will eat dinner (late) than we did last night.

______________ **15.** I ate dinner (quick) than anyone in my family, so that I could taste my cake first!

Write a Journal Entry

Imagine you are in the middle of a terrible storm. On a separate sheet of paper, write a journal entry describing what you see, hear, and feel. Use adverbs to describe when, where, and how the action happens. Underline each adverb that you use.

Notes for Home: Your child identified adverbs—words that describe verbs. ***Home Activity:*** Work with your child to list five adverbs such as *first, later, slowly, angrily,* and *far.* Take turns using each of the adverbs in a sentence.

Name ________________________________

Adverbs

RETEACHING

Read each sentence. The arrows show that **often, here,** and **happily** tell more about verbs. Underline each verb.

1. Children play often. **2.** They play here. **3.** They play happily.

A word that tells more about a verb is an **adverb**. Adverbs may tell where, when, or how an action happens.

Directions: Write whether the underlined adverb tells where, when, or how.

1. They will practice the play <u>carefully</u>. ____________

2. <u>Now</u> they paint a big sign. ____________

3. They will hang the sign <u>outside</u>. ____________

4. The tickets are sold <u>inside</u>. ____________

5. Some people bought ten tickets <u>today</u>. ____________

Directions: In each sentence, one verb that shows action is underlined. Circle the adverb. Write it on the line.

6. Many people <u>walk</u> upstairs. ________________

7. Some young children <u>run</u> around. ________________

8. The play <u>begins</u> soon. ________________

9. The audience <u>sits</u> down. ________________

10. The heavy red curtain <u>rises</u> quickly. ________________

11. The play <u>ends</u> later than we expected. ________________

12. People <u>clap</u> loudly. ________________

Notes for Home: Your child identified adverbs that tell where, when, or how. ***Home Activity:*** Look at newspaper articles and challenge your child to circle adverbs. Then have him or her draw lines from the adverbs to the verbs they modify.

Name ____

Adverbs

Directions: Circle the adverb in each sentence.

1. The people leave the harbor earlier than usual.

2. Large fishing boats take them out.

3. The large boats travel more rapidly than small boats.

4. They always carry big nets with them.

5. They drop the big nets down.

6. The crew will fish swiftly.

Directions: Complete each sentence with an adverb that answers the question in ( ).

7. The boats return to the harbor ____________________ . (When?)

8. They ____________________ bring many big fish with them. (When?)

9. The crew members catch many fish ____________________ . (How?)

10. ____________________ the crew saw a whale! (When?)

11. ____________________ many people gather. (How?)

12. They buy fresh fish ____________________ . (Where?)

13. People ____________________ like fish for dinner. (Where?)

Write a Story

On a separate sheet of paper, write a story about the ocean. Use at least four adverbs.

Notes for Home: Your child identified and used adverbs—words that tell more about verbs. ***Home Activity:*** Talk with your child about what each of you did today. Encourage your child to use adverbs in his or her statements.

Proper Nouns and Adjectives

REVIEW

Directions: Underline the word in each sentence that should be capitalized.

1. My favorite teacher is Mr. shulman.

2. I missed school on tuesday because I was sick.

3. I missed an easy test in my spanish class.

4. I live on ridge Road in a small town.

5. My house has a canadian flag out front.

6. My dad and aunt Alice were born in Canada.

7. She now lives in maine near the beach.

8. She has a dog named curly.

9. We usually visit her during august.

10. We celebrate thanksgiving together too.

Directions: Look for words that should be capitalized in each sentence. Write the sentence correctly on the line.

11. Every friday, uncle sanje comes over for dinner.

____

12. Uncle sanje was born in new delhi, India.

____

13. Now he lives in los angeles, california.

____

14. My mother and my brother ahmet cook the rice for dinner.

____

15. Rice with spicy vegetables is my favorite indian dish.

____

Notes for Home: Your child identified and capitalized proper nouns and proper adjectives. ***Home Activity:*** Make a list with your child of proper nouns, such as *Monday,* and proper adjectives, such as *Spanish*.

Name ______________________________

Capitalization

A **proper noun** names a particular person, place, or thing. All important words of a proper noun are capitalized. This includes titles and initials.

Mr. A. E. Hassim lives on an island in the East Indies.

A **proper adjective** is an adjective that is formed from a proper noun. All important words in proper adjectives are capitalized too.

Ali likes East Indian music.

In a letter, all the words of the greeting and the first word of the closing are also capitalized.

Dear Aunt Bibi,

Love always,

Directions: Read the letter Ali sent to her favorite uncle. Underline each word that should be capitalized. Rewrite these words correctly on the line.

dear uncle hassim,

sunday my mom took me to the san diego zoo.

missy and c.j. came too.

we saw an african elephant.

his name was sylvester.

will you come visit in july?

we can go to balboa park.

california is a fun place to live.

love,

ali

1. ____________________
2. ____________________
3. ____________________
4. ____________________
5. ____________________
6. ____________________
7. ____________________
8. ____________________
9. ____________________
10. ____________________

Notes for Home: Your child identified words that should always be capitalized. ***Home Activity:*** Read a newspaper article (not headlines) with your child. Have him or her circle the words that are capitalized. Then, ask your child explain why these words begin with a capital letter.

Capitalization

Directions: Unscramble the words to form a complete sentence. Write the sentence correctly on the line. Be sure to capitalize correctly.

1. to los angeles   my friend indira moved   from india.

____

2. at 22 main street,   now she lives   next to the smiths.

____

3. to see   indira can't wait   the pacific ocean.

____

4. gave her my   los angeles lakers hat.   i

____

5. mrs. anjali   spicy indian food.   cooks the best

____

Directions: Underline the words in each sentence that should be capitalized.

6. I live at 28 virginia avenue, colorado springs, co 80911.

7. Every tuesday we eat at gina's italian restaurant.

8. then we walk around the oakdale mall.

9. I sometimes buy comic books at wilson's books.

10. i always share my comic books with carrie and j.d.

Write a Paragraph

On a separate sheet of paper, write a paragraph describing a time when you shared something with a friend or family member. Be sure to capitalize words correctly.

Notes for Home: Your child capitalized proper nouns—nouns that name a particular person, place, or thing. ***Home Activity:*** Write *yes* and *no* on opposite sides of a card. Hold up one side at a time. Have your child name words that are capitalized or not *(yes—Rex; no—dog)*.

Name ______________________________ One Grain of Rice

Capitalization

RETEACHING

One sentence has a capitalization mistake. One sentence is correct. Make a check mark by the correct sentence. Rewrite the incorrect sentence correctly.

1. I enjoy watching asian elephants at the northfield zoo. __________

____

2. The African elephants are interesting too. __________

Capitalize important words of proper nouns, which name specific persons, places, or things. Capitalize proper adjectives, which are formed from proper nouns.

Directions: Read the paragraph carefully. Find capitalization mistakes in ten words. Write the words correctly on the lines.

Yesterday dan and I went to the sutherland art museum on Bixby street. Dan wanted to look at african art, and I wanted to look at art from South America. We decided to do both. First we looked at an exhibit from egypt. Then we went to another room where nigerian art was on display. After lunch we went downstairs to see argentinian art. Finally we walked across the hall to a large room where peruvian art was in glass cases. What an exciting day!

1. __________ **6.** __________

2. __________ **7.** __________

3. __________ **8.** __________

4. __________ **9.** __________

5. __________ **10.** __________

Write a Letter

Write a letter about your favorite after-school activity to someone in your class. Exchange letters with that person and check to make sure he or she used capital letters correctly.

Notes for Home: Your child identified words with mistakes in capitalization and corrected them. ***Home Activity:*** Write a letter to your child. Leave out capital letters. Read the letter together and have your child correct the mistakes in capitalization.

Name ______________________________

Capitalization

Directions: Read each phrase. In each item, circle the phrase that is capitalized correctly. Correct the phrases that have mistakes and write them on the lines.

1. dear Aunt Sarah, ______________________
   Richmond Zoo ______________________
   north America ______________________
2. French restaurant ______________________
   love, grandma ______________________
   raleigh, north carolina ______________________
3. february 18, 2002 ______________________
   Chinese music ______________________
   new york City ______________________
4. sincerely, mr. jones ______________________
   west armitage avenue ______________________
   Roy's Steak House ______________________
5. Canadian flag ______________________
   kehew book shop ______________________
   saturday, august 9 ______________________

Write Directions

On a separate sheet of paper, write directions from a friend's house to a store or other familiar place. Remember to use capital letters.

Notes for Home: Your child identified and corrected words that should begin with capital letters. ***Home Activity:*** Together, make up a poem about a favorite place or person. Have your child write the poem, using capital letters correctly.

Name ______________________________

Adverbs

REVIEW

Directions: Underline the adverb in each sentence.

1. My brother Rico and I quickly packed our backpacks.
2. We eagerly rode our bikes to the river.
3. Our raft was hidden safely behind a tree.
4. I slowly loaded our stuff on the raft.
5. I carefully put on my life jacket.
6. We paddled hard in the choppy water.
7. A hawk soared gracefully over our heads.
8. I've never seen such a beautiful sight.
9. We watched it silently.
10. Rico and I truly enjoyed our day.

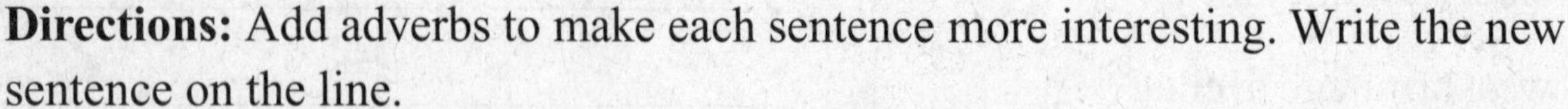

Directions: Add adverbs to make each sentence more interesting. Write the new sentence on the line.

11. The birds flew through the sky.

____

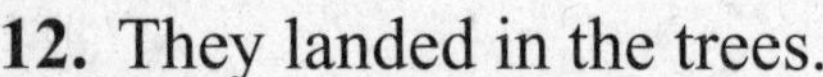

12. They landed in the trees.

____

13. Their nests were hidden.

____

14. In each nest, chicks cried for food.

____

15. The birds fed their chicks.

____

Notes for Home: Your child identified adverbs—words that describe or modify verbs—and wrote sentences with them. ***Home Activity:*** Ask your child to describe a trip to a special place using as many adverbs as possible.

Name ______________________________

Contractions

A **contraction** is a word made by putting two words together. When words are joined in a contraction, an **apostrophe (')** shows where any of the letters have been left out. Pronouns can be used with the verbs *am*, *are*, *is*, *have*, and *will* to make contractions.

I + am = I'm   you + are = you're
it + is = it's   they + have = they've   she + will = she'll

Some contractions are formed by putting a verb together with the word **not.** An **apostrophe (')** takes the place of a letter or letters.

is + not = isn't   can + not = can't   could + not = couldn't
have + not = haven't   will + not = won't

Directions: Write a word from the box that means the same as each pair of words below.

aren't	doesn't	I'm	I'll	he's	isn't	they're	we'll	weren't	won't

1. I will ______________   **6.** they are ______________

2. are not ______________   **7.** is not ______________

3. he is ______________   **8.** will not ______________

4. does not ______________   **9.** I am ______________

5. were not ______________   **10.** we will ______________

Directions: Write two words on the line that mean the same as each underlined word.

______________ **11.** I'm going to go fishing with my family at the river.

______________ **12.** We couldn't go last year because of terrible weather.

______________ **13.** But this year it's going to be beautiful.

______________ **14.** We'll catch bass, Northern pike, and maybe even some trout.

______________ **15.** I haven't ever caught a trout, but I hope to this time.

Notes for Home: Your child wrote and formed contractions. ***Home Activity:*** Make up contraction cards by writing pronouns *(I, he, she, they, we, you)* and verbs *(am, are, is, have,* and *will).* Have your child pull a card from each group and write the contraction they form.

Name ________________________________

Contractions

Directions: Write a contraction for the underlined words in each sentence.

______________ **1.** I will tell you a story I know about the ocean.

______________ **2.** I did not read about it in a book. I heard it from a captain of a ship.

______________ **3.** It is about mermaids who live in the deep sea.

______________ **4.** I have not seen one yet.

______________ **5.** That does not stop me from looking for them.

Directions: Circle the two words in each sentence that can be put together to form a contraction. Write the contraction on the line.

______________ **6.** The captain says that you are lucky if you see a mermaid.

______________ **7.** He says mermaids do not show themselves to everyone.

______________ **8.** They will only appear if you believe in them.

______________ **9.** We have looked for them through binoculars from his boat.

______________ **10.** That way, I will not miss a thing!

Write an Oral History

Think of a story you have heard about the past. It can be about your town, your family, a person, or anything else in history that has been told to you. Write down the story the way you heard it. Try to use at least three contractions. Underline each contraction you use.

Notes for Home: Your child formed contractions *(I + am = I'm* and *have + not = haven't)*. ***Home Activity:*** Read a story with your child. Together, look for any contractions. Then have your child write the two words that each contraction represents.

Name ______________________________

Contractions

One sentence uses a contraction. That sentence is shorter. Mark the sentence that uses the contraction for **we will**.

1. We will go to the circus today with Tom. ☐

2. We'll go to the circus today with Tom. ☐

A **contraction** is a shortened form of two words. Some contractions are formed from a pronoun and a verb. An apostrophe (') shows where a letter or letters are left out.

Directions: Circle the sentence in each pair that has a contraction.

1. You'll have a great time at the circus. It is so much fun.

2. It is the largest circus ever. I'm so excited.

3. I'll buy peanuts and popcorn. You will share them with me.

4. We will laugh at the clowns. They're always funny.

5. The elephant will do tricks. He's very large.

Directions: Write the contraction for each pair of underlined words.

6. <u>It is</u> time for the circus to start. ______________

7. I know <u>you will</u> love the dancing horses. ______________

8. <u>I have</u> never been to a three-ring circus. ______________

9. Now <u>I am</u> watching the bears perform. ______________

10. <u>They are</u> riding on bicycles. ______________

11. <u>You have</u> seen the last act. ______________

12. <u>We will</u> return next year. ______________

13. Now <u>we are</u> going home. ______________

Notes for Home: Your child identified and used contractions in sentences. ***Home Activity:*** Make cards for letters and apostrophes. Say pairs of words to your child *(I am, we will, he is)* and see how fast he or she can use the cards to put contractions together.

Name ______________________________

Contractions

Directions: Write the correct contraction in place of each pair of underlined words.

1. I am interested in alligators. ______________
2. I have read books about them. ______________
3. We are studying them in school. ______________
4. It is true. Alligators have webbed feet. ______________
5. They are found in warm waters. ______________
6. You will see them in most zoos. ______________
7. I will take you to see them. ______________

Directions: Underline the contraction in each sentence. Then write the two words that make the contraction.

8. Today we'll meet Suzu Hama. ______________
9. She's an expert on alligators. ______________
10. I've talked to her twice. ______________
11. She'll show us some alligators. ______________
12. Perhaps we're in time for their feeding. ______________
13. They're coming to the feeding pool now. ______________
14. You'll see everything from here. ______________
15. It's the best show at the zoo. ______________

Write a Description

On a separate sheet of paper, write a description of a zoo animal that interests you. Use contractions in your sentences.

Notes for Home: Your child used contractions of pronouns and verbs. ***Home Activity:*** Together, write a poem with contractions. Have your child rewrite the poem, this time writing both parts that make up the contractions.

Name ______________________________

REVIEW

Nouns

Directions: Underline the noun or nouns in each sentence.

1. The pilot is waiting on the runway.

2. She puts on her dark goggles and her scarf.

3. She climbs into the plane and fastens the seatbelt.

4. The engine roars loudly, and the people cheer.

5. We wave to our friend.

6. She is going to fly across both land and ocean.

7. I gave her a diary to write in and a pen.

8. She keeps them under her seat in the cockpit.

9. I hope she will land safely on the ground at the airport.

10. We all cross our fingers and wait to hear the news of her safe arrival.

Directions: Use the nouns in the box to write five different sentences. Include one or more nouns in each sentence. Try to include nouns in both the subject and the predicate.

airport	clouds	compass	jet	map	pilot	sky

11. ______________________________

12. ______________________________

13. ______________________________

14. ______________________________

15. ______________________________

Notes for Home: Your child identified nouns—words that name persons, places, or things—and used them in sentences. ***Home Activity:*** Read a movie poster or CD package with your child. Encourage your child to find nouns in the writing.

Name ____________________________________

Pronouns

A **noun** names a person, place, or thing. A **pronoun** takes the place of one or more nouns. The pronoun *I* is always capitalized.

Pronouns											
I	me	you	he	she	it	him	her	we	they	us	them

Directions: Circle the pronoun in each sentence.

1. Mary and I flew in an airplane.
2. Give the plane ticket to him.
3. Tell me about the plane trip.
4. They were flying to Texas.
5. You can even watch a movie on the plane!
6. Jason went to visit her.
7. He was leaving on Friday.
8. We are going to fly to Florida.
9. She has never been on a plane.
10. How high does it fly?

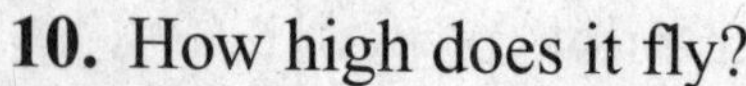

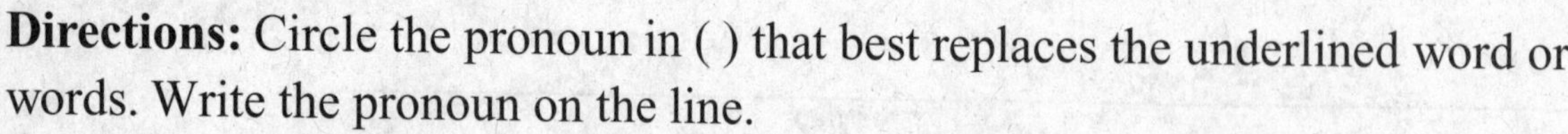

Directions: Circle the pronoun in ( ) that best replaces the underlined word or words. Write the pronoun on the line.

____________ 11. Migdalia and I visited Grandpa.(We/They)

____________ 12. Grandpa met us at the airport. (She/He)

____________ 13. There were many people in the airport. (it/them)

____________ 14. The people were all hurrying. (We/They)

____________ 15. One woman stopped to talk to Grandpa. (him/me)

Notes for Home: Your child learned common pronouns—words that take the place of nouns—and practiced using them in sentences. ***Home Activity:*** Read a story with your child. Invite your child to point out any pronouns in the story and tell what nouns they represent.

Name ______________________________

Pronouns

Directions: Draw a line that best matches each word or phrase on the left with the correct pronoun on the right.

1. Lisa and I	he
2. the boys	she
3. a box	it
4. Michael	we
5. the girl	they

Directions: Replace a word or words in the subject of each sentence with a pronoun from above. Use each pronoun only once. Write each new sentence on the line.

6. Michael and Lisa are going on a hike this weekend.

____

7. The hike will be about five miles long.

____

8. My sister and I are going too.

____

9. Lisa has hiked through the woods before.

____

10. Michael thinks Friday can't come soon enough!

____

Write a Story

On a separate sheet of paper, write a story about a boy, a girl, and a dog who go on a journey. Tell how the three travelers face something scary or dangerous and then do something brave. Be sure to mix nouns and pronouns in your story.

Notes for Home: Your child replaced nouns with pronouns and used pronouns in sentences. ***Home Activity:*** Make up sentences about people and things in your home. Encourage your child to substitute the correct pronoun for each noun you name.

Name ______________________________

Pronouns

RETEACHING

Singular Pronouns			
I	you	she	he
me	it	her	him

Plural Pronouns		
we	you	they
us	them	

Complete each sentence. Use words from the boxes above.

1. __________ found the pencils.

2. Jill found __________ .

A **pronoun** takes the place of a noun or nouns. A **singular pronoun** takes the place of a noun that names one person, place, or thing. A **plural pronoun** takes the place of a noun that names more than one person, place, or thing.

Directions: Circle two pronouns in each row.

1. see her get we red desk

2. he Mark maybe cat now I

3. but you it joy key hope

4. rug home play him Rita they

Directions: Circle the pronoun in each sentence. Write it in the space.

5. They write letters to Billy. __________

6. Matthew puts them in an envelope. __________

7. He addresses the envelope. __________

8. Alice puts it in the mailbox. __________

9. We watch the envelope drop. __________

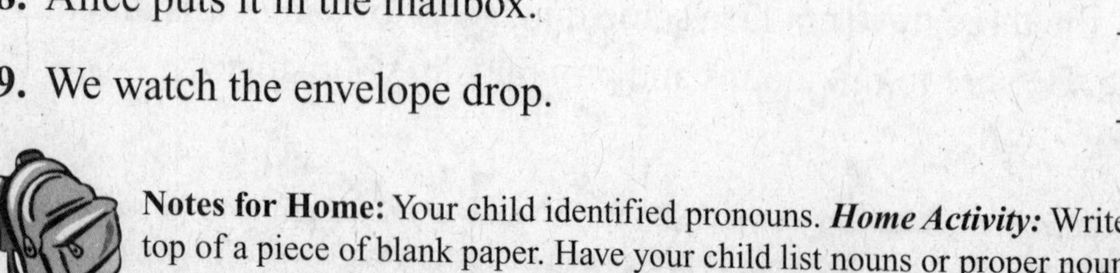

Notes for Home: Your child identified pronouns. ***Home Activity:*** Write three pronouns at the top of a piece of blank paper. Have your child list nouns or proper nouns that could replace the pronouns. (For example: *They: Mr. and Mrs. Dewey; cat and dog.*)

Name ______________________________

Pronouns

Directions: Draw a line connecting the pronouns until you reach the center of the circle. Then write the pronouns on the lines.

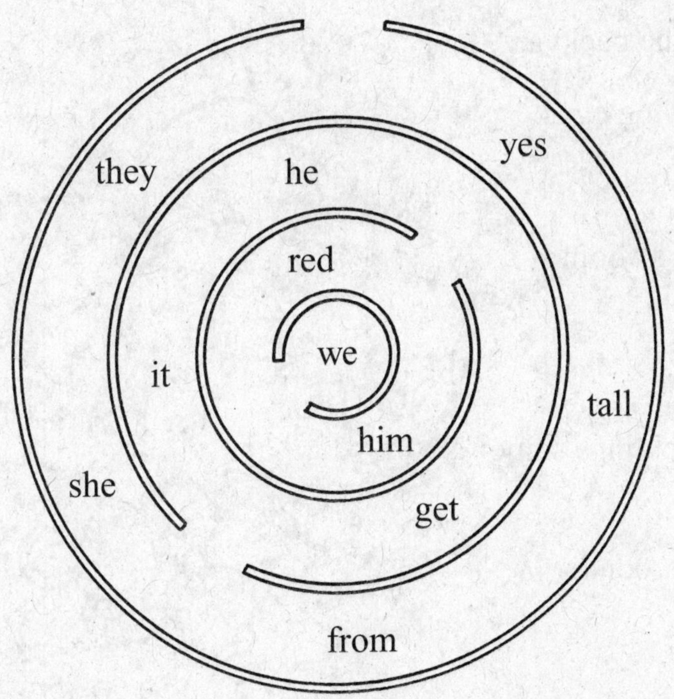

1. ____________
2. ____________
3. ____________
4. ____________
5. ____________
6. ____________

Directions: Write a correct pronoun to replace the underlined noun or nouns.

7. The tickets are for sale. ____________
8. Taro and I sell them. ____________
9. Luisa buys two tickets. ____________
10. She waits near the clock for Jim. ____________
11. The play starts in five minutes. ____________
12. Mr. Sato closes the big doors. ____________

Write a Review

Write a review of a play or story you like. Include sentences that use pronouns. Write on a separate sheet of paper.

Notes for Home: Your child identified and wrote pronouns. ***Home Activity:*** Together, choose a page from a favorite story. Point to some nouns and proper nouns and have your child say pronouns to replace them.

Pronouns

REVIEW

Directions: Underline the pronoun in each sentence.

1. The best thing happened to us yesterday.
2. Tony and I found a nest in the backyard.
3. We saw the mother duck laying eggs.
4. She laid five eggs.
5. The mother sat on them for a couple weeks.
6. Finally, they hatched.
7. I fed the mother and the ducklings some crackers.
8. The ducklings followed us around.
9. They waddled and quacked.
10. We suddenly had six new friends!

Directions: Choose the pronoun in ( ) that best replaces the underlined words. Write the pronoun on the line.

________________ **11.** Sometimes Molly and I go to the pond to feed the ducks. (they/we)

________________ **12.** The ducks are always happy to see Molly and me. (us/them)

________________ **13.** Molly and I feed the ducks stale bread. (it/them)

________________ **14.** Molly and I get the stale bread from Molly's mother. (them/it)

________________ **15.** Molly's mother works in a bakery. (She/He)

Notes for Home: Your child identified pronouns *(I, me, you, he, she, it, him, her, we, they, us, them)* and substituted pronouns for nouns in sentences. ***Home Activity:*** Read a story with your child. Encourage your child to find pronouns in the story.

Name ______________________________________

Subject and Object Pronouns

A **pronoun** can take the place of a noun. A **subject pronoun** is a pronoun used as the subject of a sentence.

We have pet ducklings.

A pronoun can also be the object in a sentence. The **object pronoun** receives the action. It goes after an action verb.

I feed them every day.

Subject Pronouns					
he	she	we	you	they	it

Object Pronouns					
him	her	us	you	them	it

Directions: Write a subject pronoun to take the place of the underlined words in each sentence.

_______________ **1.** My sister raises ducks.

_______________ **2.** Baby ducks are small and fluffy.

_______________ **3.** My sister and I like to watch them play.

_______________ **4.** Our brother built a house for the ducks.

_______________ **5.** The house is cozy and warm.

Directions: Write an object pronoun to take the place of the underlined words in each sentence.

_______________ **6.** Our mother buys duck food for my sister.

_______________ **7.** My sister gives the food to the ducks.

_______________ **8.** The ducks like my sister and me.

_______________ **9.** But the ducks really like our brother!

_______________ **10.** After all, he built the duck house.

Notes for Home: Your child used subject and object pronouns in sentences. ***Home Activity:*** Write sentences with a pronoun as the subject (*She* went to the park.) or as the object (Bud went with *her*.). Ask your child to circle the pronoun and tell whether it is a subject or object pronoun.

Name ____________________________________

Subject and Object Pronouns

Directions: Underline the pronoun in each sentence. Write **S** if the pronoun is a subject pronoun. Write **O** if the pronoun is an object pronoun.

________ **1.** I went to see the ducklings with Kenzo.

________ **2.** The park ranger takes care of them.

________ **3.** The ducklings love her.

________ **4.** We saw ducklings at the pond.

________ **5.** Kenzo wanted to feed them.

________ **6.** He had a bag of bread.

________ **7.** The ducklings crowded around us.

________ **8.** The ducklings ate all of it.

________ **9.** They quacked for more food.

________ **10.** But he didn't have any bread left!

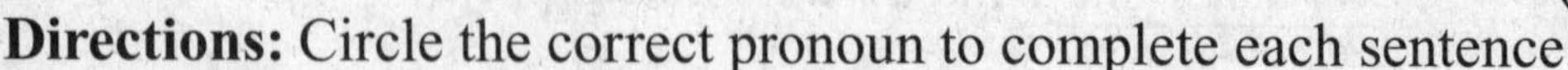

Directions: Circle the correct pronoun to complete each sentence.

11. (She/Her) is my sister.

12. Our parents gave (she/her) a puppy.

13. (Me/I) wanted a pet too.

14. Our mom gave (me/I) a parakeet.

15. Our dad gave my sister and (me/I) a fish tank.

Write a Funny Story

On a separate sheet of paper, write a funny short story about a pet or animal. It can be based on a true story or you can make it up. Use at least five subject or object pronouns.

Notes for Home: Your child identified subject pronouns—pronouns used as the subject of the sentence—and object pronouns—pronouns that receive the action. ***Home Activity:*** Have your child make a list of the subject and object pronouns he or she hears in a conversation.

Name ____________________

Subject and Object Pronouns

RETEACHING

Draw lines connecting the sentences that have meanings that match.

1. The cat follows Linda. They follow the cat.

2. The cat follows Linda and me. It follows the bike.

3. The boys follow the cat. The cat follows her.

4. The cat follows the bike. The cat follows us.

The words **I, you, she, he, it, we,** and **they** are **subject pronouns.** They are pronouns used as the subjects of sentences. The words **me, you, him, her, it, us,** and **them** are **object pronouns.** Object pronouns take the place of words in the predicates of sentences.

Directions: Circle each pronoun. Then write it.

mail me them when I run and
you open it call her he

1. ____________ **3.** ____________ **5.** ____________ **7.** ____________

2. ____________ **4.** ____________ **6.** ____________

Directions: Circle the pronoun that completes each sentence correctly.

8. (Them/They) dig the garden.

9. Sarah waters (it/him) every day.

10. Mom plants seeds in (we/it).

11. (Her/She) shows Ben the clean yard.

12. (Him/He) smiles at Mom.

13. Beans make good salads for (we/us).

Notes for Home: Your child identified subject and object pronouns. ***Home Activity:*** Write five sentences with pronouns as subjects. (For example: *They have a dog.*) Have your child circle pronouns and together, think of others that make sense in the sentences.

Name ______________________________

Subject and Object Pronouns

Directions: Circle the pronoun in each sentence. Write it on the line.

1. We have a new library in town. ____________
2. Mr. Santos likes to go to it. ____________
3. He is the new teacher. ____________
4. I look for a book about tigers. ____________
5. Xiao likes to look at folk tales with me. ____________
6. They are kept on the bottom shelf. ____________

Directions: The subject or object in each sentence is underlined. Circle the pronoun in ( ) that can take its place.

7. The door opens at nine o'clock. (I/It/They)
8. The people climb the library steps. (They/He/She)
9. Mrs. Ryan meets the children. (He/She/It)
10. José and I listen to a story. (You/They/We)
11. Sam fills a pail with shells. (them/it/you)
12. Carlos fills two pails with shells. (him/us/them)
13. Judy lets Sara fill the pail. (them/her/us)
14. At the end the children see Dad, and they all leave the beach. (him/her/them)

Write an Article

Write an article about a visit to a library. What did you see? Whom did you meet? Include pronouns in your article. Write on a separate sheet of paper.

Notes for Home: Your child identified subject and object pronouns in sentences. ***Home Activity:*** Make up sentences describing people and things in your home. Encourage your child to include pronouns in sentences. (For example: *He writes with it.*)

REVIEW

Possessive Nouns

Directions: Underline the possessive noun in each sentence.

1. Jean Babbit's father and mother are dressmakers.
2. The Babbits' dresses are beautiful.
3. He made a dress for a famous actress's party.
4. The dress's sleeves are covered in jewels.
5. Jean's mother was supposed to deliver the dress today.
6. However, the city's roads were completely covered with snow!
7. The car's tires were slipping in the snow.
8. Then, Jean thought of the twins' sled next door.
9. "We can coast down the neighbors' hill to the party." Jean said
10. Jean borrowed the children's sled and saved the day!

Directions: Use the word in ( ) to form a possessive noun to complete each sentence. Rewrite each sentence.

11. The (actresses) dresses are red. ______________________
12. (Lucy) dress was stitched carefully. ______________________
13. The (boys) sled runs fast. ______________________
14. The (wind) force was very strong. ______________________
15. The (trees) branches were broken. ______________________

Notes for Home: Your child identified possessive nouns—nouns that show ownership—and used them in sentences. ***Home Activity:*** Point out objects that belong to one or more persons. Have your child write a possessive noun to describe each object. *(This is Robert's hat.)*

Name ____________________

Possessive Pronouns

Possessive pronouns can show who or what owns, or possesses, something. Possessive pronouns can be singular or plural.

Singular Possessive Pronouns				
my	your	her	his	its
mine	yours	hers		

Kelli and I have new dresses. Her dress is beautiful. Mine is also beautiful.

Plural Possessive Pronouns		
our	your	their
ours	yours	theirs

Kelli's family makes clothes. Their dresses are famous. Are these coats yours?

Directions: Circle the possessive pronoun that best replaces the underlined word or words in each sentence.

1. Kelli sat down on Kelli's bed. (her/its)

2. Kelli put on Kelli's boots. (her/our)

3. She left Kelli's and her father's house. (your/their)

4. The wind blew the wind's cold blast. (his/its)

5. The wind blew Kelli right to Kelli's mother's house! (her/his)

Directions: Add a possessive pronoun to complete each sentence. Write the possessive pronoun on the line to the left.

____________ **6.** Kelly rubbed _____ cheeks to warm them.

____________ **7.** Kelli's stepfather welcomed _____ stepdaughter at the door.

____________ **8.** "_____ mother will give you some hot chocolate," he said.

____________ **9.** "_____ mother makes the best hot chocolate," Kelli said.

____________ **10.** "This cup is _____," said Kelli's mother as she handed the hot drink to Kelli.

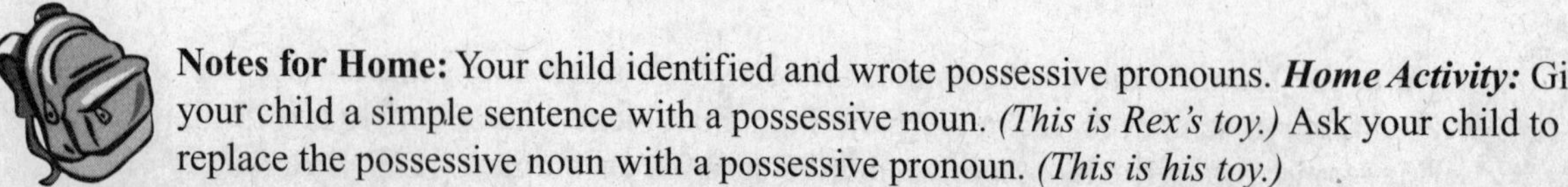

Notes for Home: Your child identified and wrote possessive pronouns. ***Home Activity:*** Give your child a simple sentence with a possessive noun. *(This is Rex's toy.)* Ask your child to replace the possessive noun with a possessive pronoun. *(This is his toy.)*

Name ______________________________

Possessive Pronouns

Directions: Write the possessive pronoun that best takes the place of the underlined word or words in each sentence. Write the possessive pronoun on the line.

______________ **1.** Mom sewed Mom's dress.

______________ **2.** It was even prettier than my dress.

______________ **3.** Then, the sewing machine blew the sewing machine's fuse.

______________ **4.** Ms. Ghupta was waiting for Ms. Ghupta's new dress.

______________ **5.** Mom was nervous because Ms. Wang and Mrs. Walsh were waiting for their dresses too.

Directions: Choose the possessive pronoun that best completes each sentence. Write the possessive pronoun on the line.

______________ **6.** Do you sew (your/yours) own clothes?

______________ **7.** I want to learn how to make (my/mine) own pants.

______________ **8.** My sisters made (her/their) dolls from socks.

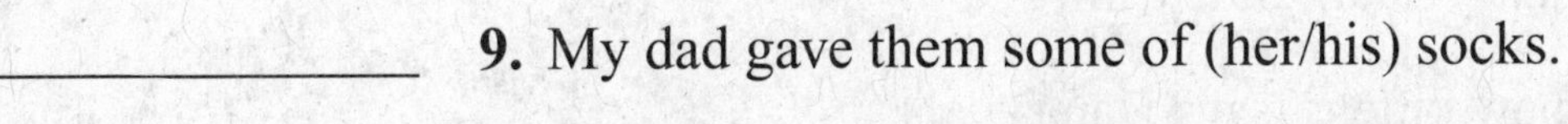

______________ **9.** My dad gave them some of (her/his) socks.

______________ **10.** I hope they don't take any of (mine/her)!

Write a Poem

On a separate sheet of paper, write a poem using the possessive pronouns you've practiced. The poem can describe some of your favorite things or a favorite season. Underline each possessive pronoun that you use.

Notes for Home: Your child used possessive pronouns—words like *my, her,* and *their*—that take the place of possessive nouns in sentences. ***Home Activity:*** Make up clues together that describe members of your family. Use possessive pronouns in the clues. *(Her hair is red.)*

Name ______________________________

Possessive Pronouns

RETEACHING

my	mine	your	yours	his	hers	her	its	our	ours	their	theirs

Complete each sentence. Write a pronoun from the box.

The girl's hair is curly.

1. ______ hair is curly.

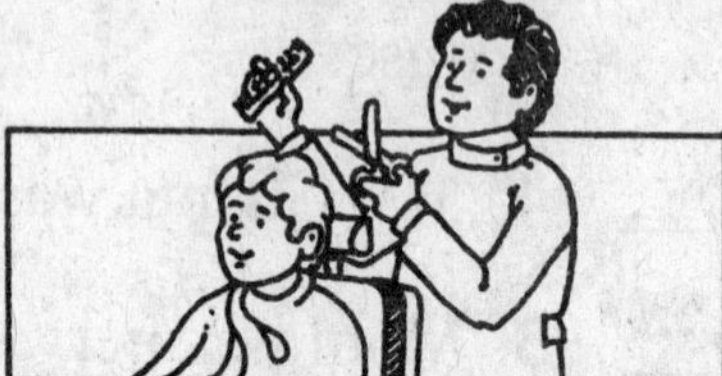

Mr. Vargas cuts the boy's hair

2. Mr. Vargas cuts ______ hair.

A **possessive pronoun** shows ownership. The words **my, mine, your, yours, his, her, hers, its, our, ours, their,** and **theirs** are possessive pronouns.

Directions: Circle the possessive pronoun in each sentence.

1. My uncle is coming to visit.

2. Uncle Nick drives his car from Boston.

3. Uncle Nick drives in front of their house.

4. Its windows have dark blue trim.

5. "Meet our new kitten," says Dana.

6. "Her name is Maxie."

7. "Maxie likes your shoelaces," laughs Dana.

8. "She looks just like ours," says Uncle Nick.

Directions: Write each possessive pronoun from the sentences above.

9. __________ **11.** __________ **13.** __________ **15.** __________

10. __________ **12.** __________ **14.** __________ **16.** __________

Notes for Home: Your child identified possessive pronouns in sentences. ***Home Activity:*** Cut out pictures from magazines or newspapers. Have your child glue them on paper and write sentences describing them. Sentences should include possessive pronouns.

Name ______________________________

Possessive Pronouns

Directions: Write the possessive pronoun from each sentence.

1. Sam likes to play his horn. ____________

2. Molly plays hers. ____________

3. Their friends play in the band too. ____________

4. "Mrs. Wong is our leader," says Sam. ____________

5. "Practice your instruments," says Mrs. Wong. ____________

Directions: Circle the possessive pronoun in ( ) that takes the place of the underlined words. Then write the pronouns on the music stands.

6. Mary's teacher has a new piano. (His/Her/Its)

7. The movers delivered Mr. Lamb's piano last week. (his/her/its)

8. The movers' truck was very big. (His/Their/My)

9. The piano's keys are black and white and shiny. (Her/Yours/Its)

10. The students' faces light up. (Their/Its/My)

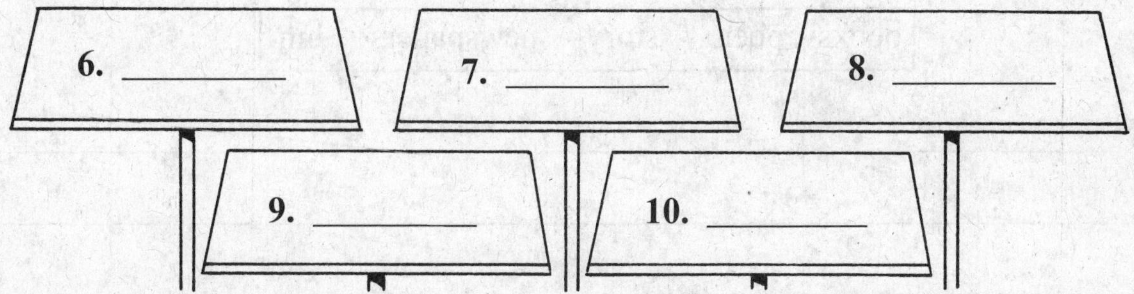

Write a Song

Write a song about an instrument you like. Use some possessive pronouns. Write on a separate sheet of paper.

Notes for Home: Your child wrote and identified possessive pronouns—pronouns that show ownership—in sentences. ***Home Activity:*** Make up a song about objects family members own. Use possessive pronouns. (For example: *This is his toy airplane.*)

Name ______________________________

Objects

REVIEW

Directions: Underline the object—the word or words that identify the receiver of the action—in each sentence.

1. Bobby visits the library.
2. He chooses a book.
3. Bobby finds a seat.
4. Bobby reads the story.
5. He turns the pages quickly.
6. Soon, he finishes the last page.

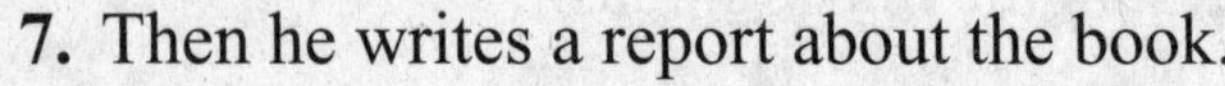

7. Then he writes a report about the book.

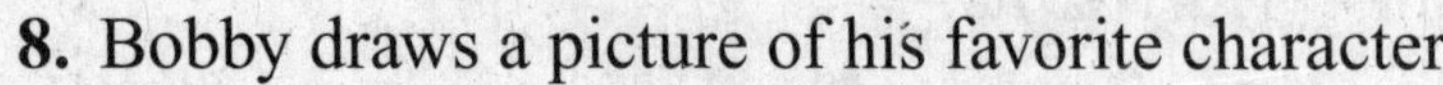

8. Bobby draws a picture of his favorite character.

9. He folds it like a book cover.

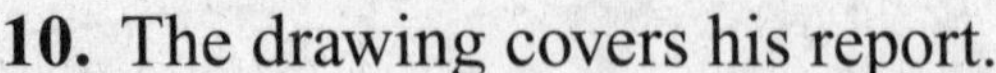

10. The drawing covers his report.

Directions: For each word in the box, write a sentence that uses that word as the object, the receiver of the action.

books	poem	story	newspapers	him

11. ______________________________

12. ______________________________

13. ______________________________

14. ______________________________

15. ______________________________

Notes for Home: Your child identified and used objects (nouns or pronouns that follow action verbs and receive the action). ***Home Activity:*** Give a subject and an action verb. Ask your child to give a noun or a pronoun that receives the action. *(She lifts the box.)*

Name ____

Prepositions

A **preposition** is a word that shows a relationship between a noun or pronoun and another word or words in a sentence: I read a book <u>about</u> dogs.

A preposition is the first word in a **prepositional phrase.** A prepositional phrase can act like an adjective or adverb.

I live in a house <u>with a red roof</u>.	This phrase describes the house.
Jim lives <u>near the public library</u>.	This phrase tells where Jim lives.

Common Prepositions
after at before behind by down for from in near of on to with

Directions: Circle the preposition in each sentence.

1. My dad was raised in a cabin.
2. The cabin was near a mill.
3. My dad worked at the mill.
4. He read from hand-me-down books.
5. He studied his books before his bedtime each night.
6. Sometimes he read by candlelight.
7. Today he works at a good job.
8. That is what hard work can do for you.

Directions: Choose a preposition that makes the most sense in each sentence. Write the preposition on the line to the left.

________________ 9. I study _____ the porch.

________________ 10. My mother reads to me _____ dinner.

________________ 11. Last night I read a book _____ Fran's house.

________________ 12. Fran lives _____ the street.

________________ 13. The book was a present _____ my birthday.

________________ 14. Fran sat _____ the floor and listened.

________________ 15. Now she wants a copy _____ the book.

Notes for Home: Your child identified and used prepositions—words that relate a word or phrase to other words. Some prepositions are: *in, about, by, on, before, to,* and *near.* ***Home Activity:*** Using the list of prepositions, ask your child to use each preposition in a sentence.

Name ______________________________

Prepositions

Directions: Choose the preposition from the box that best completes each sentence. Write the prepositions on the matching numbered lines below. You can use words more than once.

about	after	around	at	for	in	near	on	to	under	with

1. _____ a long day at school, Kenya goes **2.** _____ the public library **3.** _____ her house. First, she looks **4.** _____ the books **5.** _____ the non-fiction section. Kenya picks out a book **6.** _____ Booker T. Washington. Kenya checks out the book **7.** _____ the front desk and heads home.

First, Kenya eats dinner **8.** _____ her family. **9.** _____ dinner she sits down **10.** _____ her favorite chair. She puts her feet **11.** _____ the foot stool and starts her new book. She reads until it is time **12.** _____ bed. Kenya brings her book **13.** _____ bed. She climbs **14.** _____ the covers and starts to read again. Soon, she falls asleep and dreams **15.** _____ meeting Booker T. Washington.

1. __________	**6.** __________	**11.** __________
2. __________	**7.** __________	**12.** __________
3. __________	**8.** __________	**13.** __________
4. __________	**9.** __________	**14.** __________
5. __________	**10.** __________	**15.** __________

Write a Paragraph

On a separate sheet of paper, write a paragraph describing an event from a book you have read. Underline the prepositions you use.

Notes for Home: Your child identified and used prepositions—words, such as *in, about, by,* and *near,* that relate a word or phrase to other words. ***Home Activity:*** Read a paragraph from a story with your child. Invite your child to identify the prepositions in the paragraph.

Name ______________________________

Prepositions

RETEACHING

Read the sentences. Circle the prepositions.

1. The cat ran up the tree.
2. I stood behind him.

A **preposition** shows a relationship between words in a sentence. It is the first word of a prepositional phrase.

Directions: Draw a line connecting the prepositions. Find your way out of the maze.

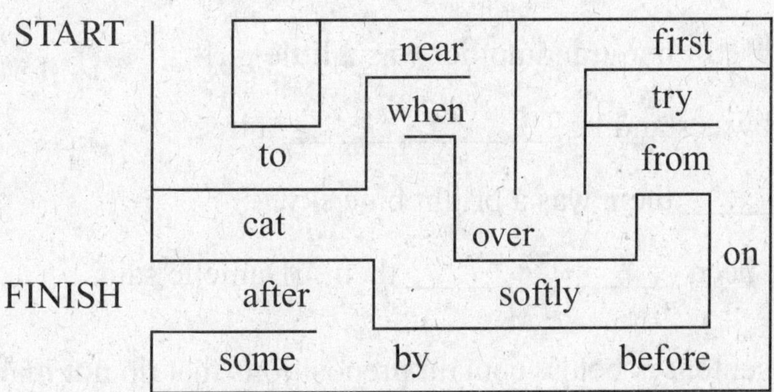

Directions: Choose the preposition in ( ) that correctly completes the sentence. Write the preposition on the line.

1. My brother and I walk (over/slowly) the bridge. __________
2. We try not to stand (touch/near) the edge. __________
3. He always laughs (sometimes/at) the way the bridge creaks. __________
4. Sometimes we race (across/quickly) the bridge. __________
5. It's narrow, so one person has to go (always/behind) the other. __________
6. When I go fishing, I always take him (later/with) me. __________

Notes for Home: Your child identified and wrote prepositions. (For example: *over, under, about*) ***Home Activity:*** Create a four-box comic strip with your child. Challenge him or her to use prepositions and write captions.

Name ___________________________________

Prepositions

Directions: Choose a preposition from the box that makes sense in the sentence. Write it on the line.

about	above	at	behind	below	by	down	near	over	to	up	with

1. Danielle found a book ______________ dogs.
2. She found it ______________ a stack of old magazines.
3. Also ______________ the book was a photograph of some people.
4. When she looked ______________ the photograph, she recognized her grandmother.
5. ______________ her grandmother was a little girl.
6. The little girl was standing ______________ a tree.
7. ______________ them was a bright blue sky.
8. "I wish I had been ______________ them," Danielle said.

Directions: The sentences below contain prepositions that do not make sense. Rewrite each sentence with a preposition that makes sense in the sentence.

9. Stuart was walking with the river.

____

10. He noticed the sky below his head.

____

11. "What a beautiful day," he said about his brother.

____

12. Richard said, "It is nice to live under a river."

____

Notes for Home: Your child identified and wrote prepositions. ***Home Activity:*** Ask your child for some examples of prepositions. Have him or her explain how they are used.

Name ___________________________________

Compound Subjects, Predicates, and Sentences

REVIEW

Directions: Combine the **subjects** of Sentences A and B to complete Sentence C.

1. Sentence A: Aaron rides horses. Sentence B: Marcos rides horses.

Sentence C: __________ and __________ ride horses.

2. Sentence A: Susie is in my riding class. Sentence B: Heidi is in my riding class.

Sentence C: __________ and __________ are in my riding class.

3. Sentence A: Susie brushes the horses every day. Sentence B: I brush the horses every day.

Sentence C: __________ and __________ brush the horses every day.

Directions: Combine the **predicates** of Sentences A and B to complete Sentence C.

4. Sentence A: Tony's horse gallops. Sentence B: Tony's horse jumps.

Sentence C: Tony's horse __________ and __________.

5. Sentence A: My family lives on a farm. Sentence B: My family works on a farm.

Sentence C: My family __________ and __________ on a farm.

6. Sentence A: I feed the horses. Sentence B: I wash the horses.

Sentence C: I __________ and __________ the horses.

Directions: Each sentence below combines two shorter sentences. Underline each shorter sentence.

7. I like riding horses, and my sister likes drawing them.

8. The horses live in the stable, and the pigs live in the pen.

9. We went to the state fair, and my dad bought a new horse.

10. I named the horse Flash, and my sister braided her mane.

Notes for Home: Your child combined subjects and predicates and identified shorter sentences within compound sentences. ***Home Activity:*** Make up pairs of sentences similar to sentences A and B above. Ask your child to combine the subjects or the predicates.

Conjunctions

A **conjunction** connects words or groups of words. *And, but,* and *or* are common conjunctions.
To add information, use *and:* The farmhouse is old <u>and</u> run down.
To show a choice, use *or:* We can stay here <u>or</u> move away.
To show a difference, use *but:* I like ponies, <u>but</u> my brother doesn't.

Directions: Circle the conjunction in each sentence.

1. Yoshi lived with her mother and father.

2. She loved animals, but her parents didn't.

3. Yoshi said she would feed it and care for it.

4. Her parents said she could have a cat, but not a dog.

5. Yoshi would get either a gray cat or a black cat.

Directions: Circle the conjunction that best completes each sentence. Write the conjunction on the line.

________ **6.** We live on a farm (or/and) have a lot of animals.

________ **7.** I am young (but/or) I help when I can.

________ **8.** I can feed the pigs (but/and) the goats.

________ **9.** I feed the chickens (but/and) pick up the eggs.

________ **10.** Someday I'll either be a farmer (or/but) a teacher.

________ **11.** My sister (or/and) I both like to ride horses.

________ **12.** We will go riding either this Saturday (and/or) next.

________ **13.** We wanted to ride last weekend, (or/but) the weather was bad.

________ **14.** My sister wants to be either a vet (or/but) a rodeo star.

________ **15.** I love our farm (but/and) my family too.

Notes for Home: Your child identified and used the conjunctions *and, but,* and *or.* ***Home Activity:*** Write the words *and, but,* and *or* on separate slips of paper and place them in a hat or a bowl. Ask your child to draw a slip of paper and use that conjunction in a sentence.

Name ___________________________________

Conjunctions

Directions: Choose the conjunction from the box that best completes each sentence. Write the conjunction on the matching numbered lines to the right.

and
but
or

Callie **1.** _____ Corey are twins. They look alike, **2.** _____ they are very different. They like to do different things. Callie likes horseback riding **3.** _____ Corey doesn't. He prefers to read and draw.

One day Callie told Corey either he could come riding with her **4.** _____ he could stay home. Corey decided to stay home, **5.** _____ later he changed his mind.

Corey ran to the stable **6.** _____ saw Callie. "Are you going to ride **7.** _____ are you going to watch?" Callie asked him. Corey said he would watch, **8.** _____ all his friends laughed at him. "You're afraid to ride!" they said.

Corey got mad **9.** _____ jumped on Callie's horse. He almost fell, **10.** _____ he managed to stay on. Soon he was riding with everyone else. "This is fun!" he yelled.

1. __________

2. __________

3. __________

4. __________

5. __________

6. __________

7. __________

8. __________

9. __________

10. __________

Write a Comparison

On a separate sheet of paper, write a list that compares yourself to a friend or family member. Use conjunctions to list the things that make you the same and the things that make you different from one another.

Notes for Home: Your child used the conjunctions *and, but,* and *or* in sentences. ***Home Activity:*** Challenge your child to draw pictures that illustrate the conjunctions *and, but,* and *or.* Have your child write a sentence under each picture.

Name ______________________________

Conjunctions

RETEACHING

Circle the conjunction in each sentence.

1. I wrote a poem and a song. **2.** He likes pizza, but he doesn't like spaghetti.

Words like **and, but,** and **or** are conjunctions. They are used to connect words or groups of words. **And** shows adding information, **or** shows a choice, and **but** shows a difference.

Directions: Choose a conjunction from the box that makes sense in each sentence. Write it on the line.

and	but	or

1. My parents speak Italian, __________ I like to listen to them.
2. They speak it well, __________ I do not.
3. After dinner Dad either tells stories __________ sings songs.
4. My mother's spaghetti sauce is good, __________ my grandmother's is better.
5. I like to eat dinner at my grandparents' house, __________ I do it every Saturday.
6. We stay up late __________ tell stories.
7. I like to sleep late, __________ my brother wakes me early.
8. He gets up early __________ plays in my room.
9. Sometimes he throws a pillow at me __________ jumps on my bed.
10. Dad comes in __________ asks us to stop.

Notes for Home: Your child identified conjunctions—words such as *but, and,* and *or*—in sentences. ***Home Activity:*** Read magazine or newspaper articles. Challenge your child to find conjunctions in sentences.

Name ____________________

Conjunctions

Directions: Finish each sentence by adding a conjunction and more information.

1. Some mornings I walk the dog ____________________

2. They like boats ____________________

3. Tim usually leaves early ____________________

4. I have never tried Japanese food ____________________

5. Deirdre enjoys singing ____________________

6. Troy collected seashells ____________________

7. We hike on the hard trail ____________________

8. Every summer my family cleans the garage ____________________

9. Dad is either ice fishing ____________________

10. Donna dislikes swimming ____________________

11. Russ started out playing the trombone ____________________

12. The band plays fast songs ____________________

13. Sometimes my friends visit me ____________________

14. Five people in my class are good artists ____________________

15. Janette used the Internet ____________________

16. They bring their own food ____________________

17. He stepped in puddles ____________________

18. At night we all read books ____________________

Write an Advertisement

Compare two objects, such as two kinds of food or two kinds of shoes, and write an advertisement telling why one is better than the other. Use the conjunctions **and**, **but**, and **or** to compare the objects.

Notes for Home: Your child used conjunctions—words such as *but, and,* and *or*—to finish sentences. ***Home Activity:*** Say pairs of sentences to your child and ask him or her to use conjunctions to combine them.

Name ______________________________

Compound Subjects and Predicates

REVIEW

Directions: Underline the compound subject in each sentence.

1. Anna and Luis had a party.
2. Clowns and jugglers were at the party.
3. Candy and party favors fell from the piñatas.
4. Luis's family and Anna's family sang a song.
5. The cake and ice cream were gone in a flash!

Directions: Underline the compound predicate in each sentence.

6. We all ate and talked.
7. Luis laughed and sang.
8. He made hats and built piñatas.
9. We hit the piñatas and broke them open.
10. All the children ran and grabbed the treats.

Directions: Write a compound subject or predicate to complete each sentence.

11. ____________________ were invited to the party.
12. ______________________ gave Anna a necklace.
13. Luis ____.
14. After the party, we ____________________________________.
15. I ____.

Notes for Home: Your child identified and wrote compound subjects *(Maria and Jenny laughed.)* and compound predicates *(The wind blew and howled.)*. ***Home Activity:*** Make up a list of subjects and verbs. Take turns making up sentences with compound subjects and predicates.

Name ________________________________

Review of Sentences

A **sentence** is a group of words that tells, asks, commands, or exclaims.

Chris has a new hat.

You can tell whether a group of words is a sentence by checking to see if it expresses a complete thought.

Sentence: He got it as a gift.
Not a Sentence: Got it as a gift.

Directions: Write **S** if each group of words is a complete sentence. Write **NS** if the group of words is not a complete sentence.

________ **1.** Pedro wore his new hat.

________ **2.** To visit Gina.

________ **3.** A windy day.

________ **4.** A dog barked.

________ **5.** The hat blew away.

________ **6.** Ran after the hat.

________ **7.** He could not catch it.

________ **8.** Pedro was.

________ **9.** Was waiting in front of her house.

________ **10.** Gina wore the new hat.

Directions: For each group of words above that is not a sentence, add words to make it a complete sentence. Write the new sentences on the lines.

11. ____

12. ____

13. ____

14. ____

15. ____

Notes for Home: Your child identified and wrote complete sentences. ***Home Activity:*** Write some simple sentences on a long strip of paper. Cut the sentences into pieces. Have your child arrange the pieces into complete sentences.

Name ______________________________

Review of Sentences

Directions: Draw a line to connect the word or words in the **Who or What** column with a group of words in the **What Happened** column to form a complete sentence. Make sure each sentence makes sense. Write the new sentences on the lines.

Who or What	What Happened
1. Tonight, my family	made her famous tacos.
2. The tables	were swinging at the piñata.
3. The moon	licked my plate.
4. Crickets	were filled with food.
5. Moths	had a fiesta at our house.
6. Blindfolded children	played music together.
7. My mom	wanted to go home.
8. Our dog	chirped in the tall grass.
9. The band	fluttered around the lanterns.
10. No one	was full in the sky.

____

____

____

____

____

Write a Paragraph

On a separate sheet of paper, write a paragraph describing a fun party. Be sure to use all complete sentences.

Notes for Home: Your child formed sentences from sentence fragments, or incomplete sentences. ***Home Activity:*** Write three fragments. (For example: *The boy* or *To the beach*) Ask your child to turn each fragment into a complete sentence.

Name ______________________

RETEACHING

Review of Sentences

Make a check mark by the complete sentence.

1. Across the field of flowers. ☐
2. She showed me photos of her trip. ☐
3. Fifty times without a miss. ☐

A **sentence** is a group of words that tells, asks, commands, or exclaims. It begins with a capital letter and ends with an end mark.

Directions: Circle the complete sentences. Add more words to the incomplete sentences and write the new sentences on the lines.

1. Jean smiles at her.
2. Smiles back at Jean.
3. The pencil sharpener.
4. The class is friendly.
5. The teacher arrives.
6. To start the class.
7. ______________________
8. ______________________
9. ______________________

Directions: Write **sentence** if the group of words is a complete sentence. Write **not a sentence** if the group of words is not a complete sentence.

10. The teacher writes his name. ______________
11. After the school bell. ______________
12. The children tell stories. ______________
13. Lots of fun on vacation. ______________

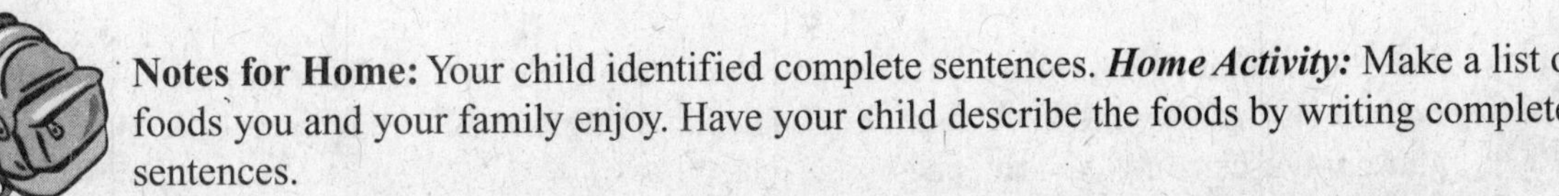

Notes for Home: Your child identified complete sentences. ***Home Activity:*** Make a list of foods you and your family enjoy. Have your child describe the foods by writing complete sentences.

Name ________________________________

Review of Sentences

Directions: Find and circle the complete sentences below. Remember that a **sentence** is a group of words that tells, asks, commands, or exclaims. It expresses a complete thought.

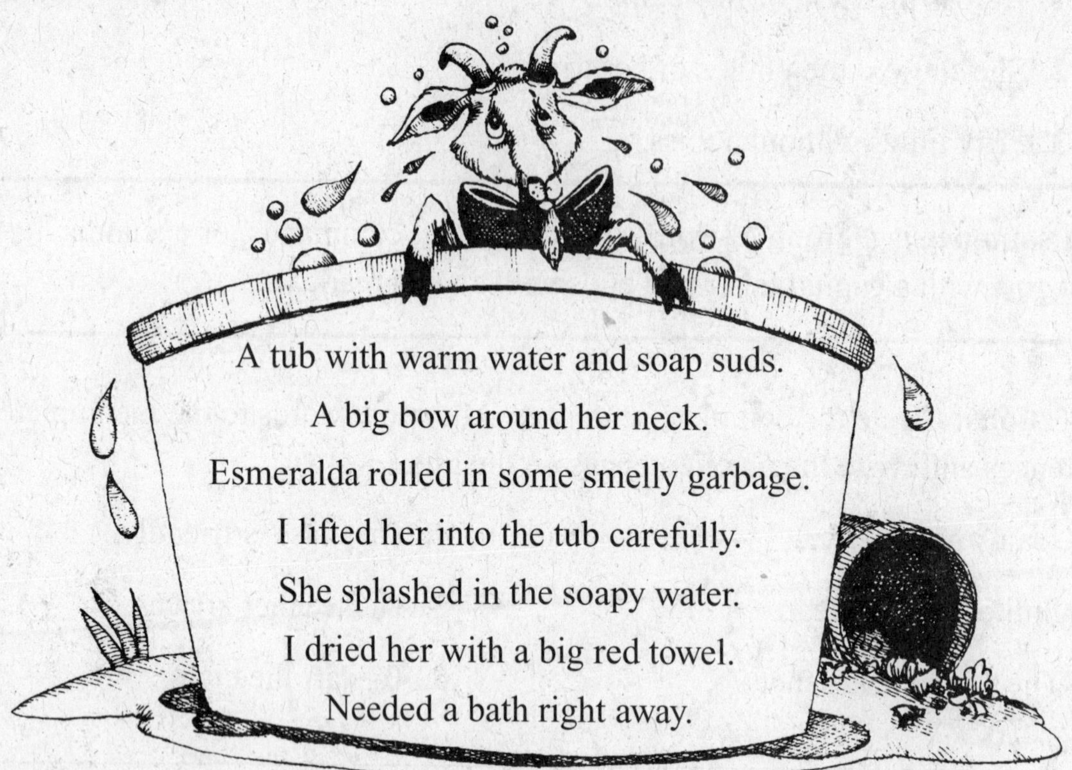

A tub with warm water and soap suds.

A big bow around her neck.

Esmeralda rolled in some smelly garbage.

I lifted her into the tub carefully.

She splashed in the soapy water.

I dried her with a big red towel.

Needed a bath right away.

Directions: Write your own tale about Esmeralda. Use some of the complete sentences above and other sentences you make up. Make sure you put them in an order that makes sense.

____

____

____

____

____

____

Notes for Home: Your child identified and wrote complete sentences. ***Home Activity:*** Read food labels together and have your child make up a jingle to advertise the foods. Make sure your child uses complete sentences.

Name ________________________________

REVIEW

Conjunctions

Directions: Underline the conjunction in each sentence.

1. My older sister Barb will visit our aunt and uncle.

2. They told Barb she could visit on Saturday or Sunday.

3. She could take a train, but she doesn't have any money.

4. Barb wants to get a job baby-sitting or cleaning.

5. Barb called some of our friends and neighbors.

6. Barb knocked on doors and put up flyers.

7. She waited by the phone, but no one called.

8. Finally, a woman called and asked Barb to baby-sit.

9. The woman needed a baby-sitter for Friday or Saturday.

10. Barb baby-sat on Friday and visited our relatives on Saturday.

Directions: Combine each pair of sentences into one sentence. Use *and, but,* or *or* to form a compound subject or compound predicate. Write the sentence on the line.

11. I wrote a letter to my best friend Peggy. I mailed a letter to my best friend Peggy.

____

12. She moved. She now lives in another town.

____

13. I will see Peggy next weekend. I will see Peggy the following weekend.

____

14. My friend Sally will take a train to see Peggy. I will take a train to see Peggy.

____

15. We will leave on a Friday. We will return on a Sunday.

____

Notes for Home: Your child identified and used conjunctions *(and, or,* or *but)* in sentences. ***Home Activity:*** Ask your child to explain when to use *and, or,* and *but* to connect words or groups of words. Have your child use each conjunction in a sentence.

Name ______________________________

Compound Sentences

You can combine two related sentences into one **compound sentence.** Write the first sentence. Put a comma in the place of the end punctuation. Use a conjunction such as *and* to join the first and second sentence. Begin the second sentence with a small letter unless the first word is a proper noun, a proper adjective, or the pronoun *I*.

Mary visited her grandparents.
They met her at the train station.
→ Mary visited her grandparents, and they met her at the train station.

Mary stepped off the train.
Her grandfather hugged her.
→ Mary stepped off the train, and her grandfather hugged her.

Directions: Use a comma and the conjunction *and* to combine each pair of sentences into one compound sentence. Write the new sentence on the line.

1. The train pulled out of the station. I waved good-bye.

____

2. The train sped on. The trees whizzed by.

____

3. I got my ticket out of my bag. The conductor took it.

____

4. My seat was very comfortable. I took a short nap.

____

5. The dining car was open. I ate a good dinner.

____

Notes for Home: Your child used the conjunction *and* to combine sentences. ***Home Activity:*** Write several simple sentences. Have your child try to combine two sentences into one sentence *(I sang. The band played music. I sang, and the band played music.)*.

Name ______________________

Compound Sentences

Directions: Use a comma and the conjunction *and* to combine each pair of underlined sentences into one compound sentence. Write the new sentences below.

Dear Grandpa,

What's new? **1.** We all miss you. Jim and I want to visit. **2.** We want to come by train. Mom and Dad said we could. **3.** I am saving money. Jim is trying to save too. **4.** I last saw you at Thanksgiving. You had a new puppy. **5.** Rocky is so cute. We are excited to see him. We'll see you soon.

Love,

Maggie

1. ______________________
2. ______________________
3. ______________________
4. ______________________
5. ______________________

Write a Postscript

On a separate sheet of paper, write a postscript to Maggie's letter. A postscript comes after the signature and begins with P.S. Try to include one or more sentences that use *and* to combine two shorter sentences.

Notes for Home: Your child used a comma and the conjunction *and* to combine two short sentences into one compound sentence. ***Home Activity:*** Read some sentences from a news story aloud to your child and ask whether or not they are compound sentences.

Name ____________________

Compound Sentences

RETEACHING

Combine the sentences to make one sentence.

The tale was funny. The hero was a duck.

____

A **compound sentence** is made by joining two sentences together. Remember to use a comma before the word **and** to combine two sentences that go together.

Directions: Combine each pair of sentences with a comma and the word **and.**

1. Cartoons are funny. We all enjoy them.

____

2. They are easy to draw. Anyone can learn.

____

3. Some have words. Others are just pictures.

____

4. We have a bulletin board. I pin pictures on it.

____

5. Rosanna thinks of funny words. Juan prints them.

____

6. Dad brings me art supplies. I draw every day.

____

Notes for Home: Your child used commas and the word *and* to form compound sentences. ***Home Activity:*** Say a sentence. Have your child use your sentence and other words to create a compound sentence.

Name ______________________________

Compound Sentences

Directions: Combine each pair of sentences. Remember to use a comma before the word **and** to combine two sentences that go together.

My grandmother left school. She worked to support her family.

____

____

During the day she sewed dresses. At night she took care of her younger sisters.

____

____

She studied on her own. She taught herself English.

____

At last her father stopped working at night. Grandma was able to go to school.

____

____

Grandma graduated with honors. She became a nurse at a hospital.

____

____

Today she is seventy years old. Everyone still depends on her.

____

____

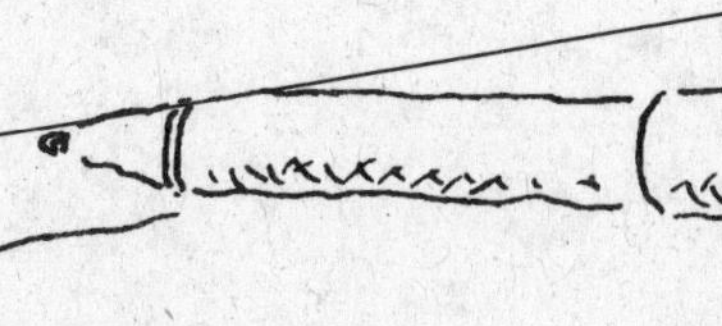

Notes for Home: Your child used commas and the word *and* to combine two sentences that go together. ***Home Activity:*** Start a sentence *(She walked down the stairs, . . .)* and have your child finish it, using the word *and. (. . . and she spoke to her brother.)*

Name ____________________

Sentence Punctuation

REVIEW

Directions: Read this conversation between a mother and her sons. Write the correct punctuation mark at the end of each sentence.

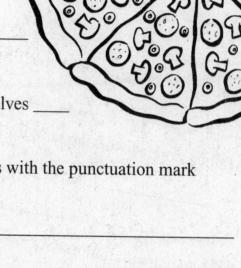

1. Mom: I want you boys to make dinner tonight ____
2. Billy: Do we have to make it tonight ____
3. Joey: What will we make ____
4. Mom: Use your imagination ____
5. Billy: What if we made cookies ____
6. Joey: That's a great idea ____
7. Mom: I mean a real dinner ____
8. Billy and Joey: Let's make pizza ____
9. Mom: Do you need my help ____
10. Billy and Joey: We can do it ourselves ____

Directions: Write a sentence that ends with the punctuation mark given in ( ).

11. (period) ____________________
12. (question mark) ____________________
13. (exclamation mark) ____________________
14. (question mark) ____________________
15. (period) ____________________

Notes for Home: Your child punctuated and wrote sentences. ***Home Activity:*** Draw a question mark, period, and exclamation mark on three separate sheets of paper. Have your child make up a sentence to match each type of punctuation mark you hold up.

Name ______________________________

Commas

Use a comma and a conjunction to join two sentences.

It was time to eat, and I was hungry.

Use commas to separate words in a series.

Marie, Anne, and Lisa are in the kitchen.

Use a comma to separate the month and day from the year and to separate the year from the rest of the sentence.

Mickey was born on April 1, 1991. On April 1, 2011, Mickey will be twenty years old.

Use a comma between the names of a street, city, and state abbreviation in an address and after the name of the state in a sentence. Never put a comma between a state abbreviation and a zip code.

Jan lives at 56 Bay Road, Orlando, FL 32887.
Jan has lived in Orlando, Florida, for two years.

Directions: Add a comma or commas to correct each sentence.

1. We will buy the food and Dad will cook it.
2. Dad will cook and Ramon will help.
3. Lucy likes broccoli and Nathaniel likes asparagus.
4. Everything on the table is red white and blue.
5. My favorite fruits are pears apples bananas and plums.
6. Sam Connie and Ray will be here soon.
7. On February 12 1809 Abraham Lincoln was born.
8. The Declaration of Independence was signed on July 4 1776.
9. I am moving to Little Rock Arkansas next month.
10. Is Lee's address 113 Maple Street Madison WI 53705?

Notes for Home: Your child inserted commas in compound sentences, in series, in dates, and in addresses. ***Home Activity:*** Have your child use the addresses of friends and family or the dates of special events in sentences. Talk about where to place commas.

Name ____

Commas

Directions: Add a comma or commas to correct each sentence.

1. I wanted to have a party and my mom said it was okay.
2. She wrote out the invitations and I stuck on the stamps.
3. The party was to celebrate the day I got adopted on May 2 1998.
4. I put this return address on each envelope: 1212 Oak Street Underhill VT 05489.
5. I asked my guests to come at 3 o'clock on May 2 2000.
6. Dennis was in Dallas Texas on vacation.
7. Everyone else said they'd come and I was glad.
8. I bought strawberries carrot cake and frozen yogurt.
9. I put the frozen yogurt in the freezer and the cake and the berries went on the table.
10. The doorbell rang and I answered it.

Directions: On each line below, write a sentence that includes a comma. Be sure to use commas correctly.

11. ____
12. ____
13. ____
14. ____
15. ____

Write a Thank-You Note

On a separate sheet of paper, write a note thanking a friend for serving you a delicious meal. Include a date and an address. Be sure to use commas correctly.

Notes for Home: Your child inserted commas in compound sentences (two sentences combined into one), words in a series, dates, and addresses. ***Home Activity:*** Write dates and addresses on a sheet of paper. Ask your child to insert the commas. *(Monday, July 4, 1776).*

Name ________________________

RETEACHING

Commas

Read the sentences. In each pair, circle the sentence in which commas are used correctly.

1. Sally Jean Fred and Mike laughed.
2. Sally, Jean, Fred, and Mike laughed.
3. He learned to read and he tried to teach his sister.
4. He learned to read, and he tried to teach his sister.
5. I was born on October 27 1992 in Memphis TN.
6. I was born on October 27, 1992, in Memphis, TN.

Commas help make ideas clear. Use commas to separate words in a series. Use commas to combine sentences. Use a comma to separate the month and day from the year and to separate the year from the rest of the sentence.

Directions: Put commas in each sentence where they are needed.

1. Paul Kim and Eva read about Richard E. Byrd.
2. He was an explorer and he loved adventure travel.
3. Lindsay was born on March 8 1994 in Maine.
4. She likes to read books about penguins cats and buildings.
5. Kazuo likes swimming and he tries to learn new things.
6. He traveled on boats sleds and airplanes.
7. On August 27 2000 he swam four miles.
8. Josh uses pencils pens and markers to create his designs.
9. He enjoys painting pictures and he sells them at an art fair.

Notes for Home: Your child used commas in sentences. ***Home Activity:*** Discuss a family get-together, including the date it took place. Have your child write a description of it, using commas correctly.

Name ______________________________

Commas

Directions: Proofread the postcard. Remember to use **commas** to separate three or more items in a series. Also use a comma to separate the parts of a compound sentence.

1.–9.

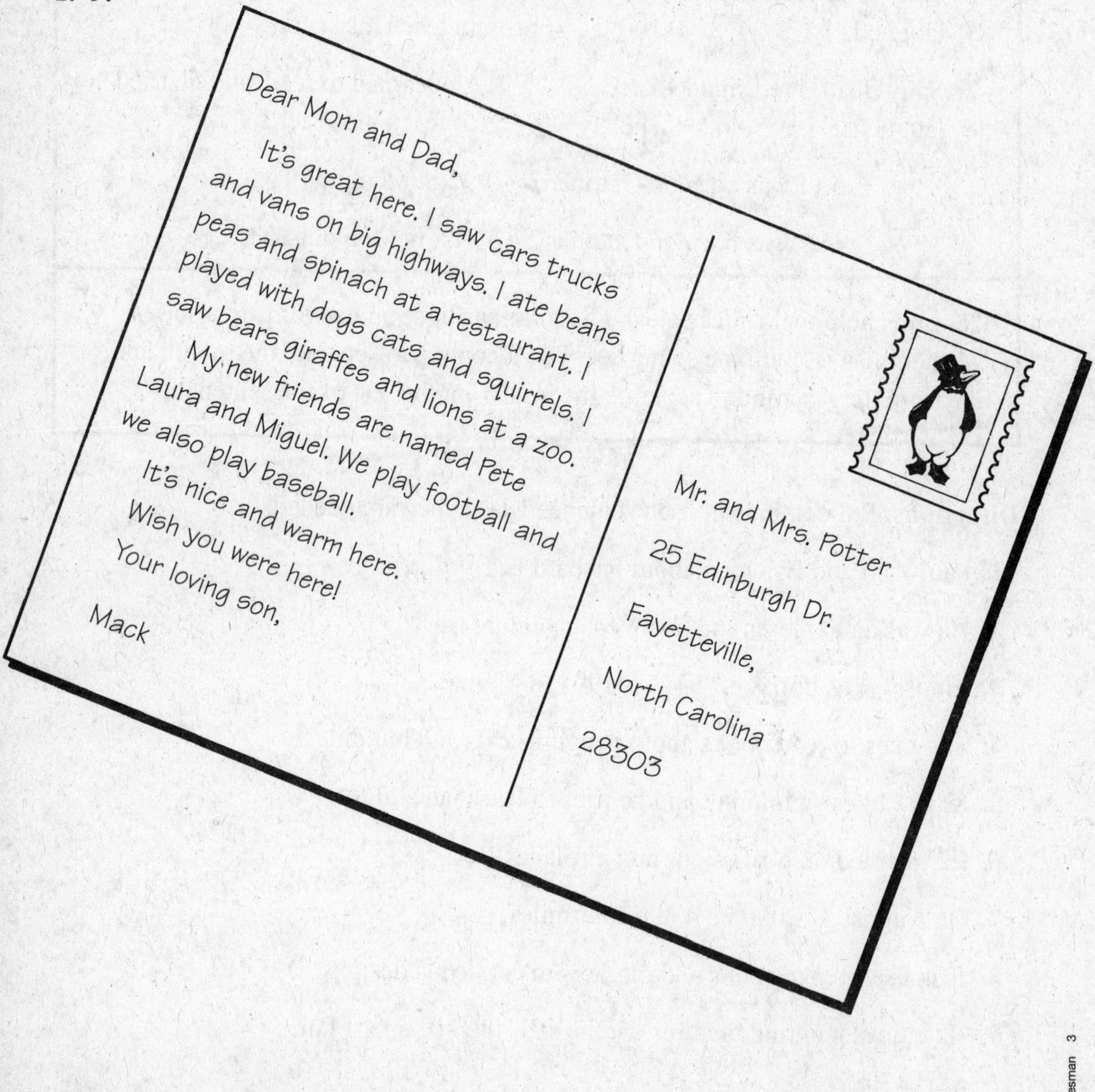

Dear Mom and Dad,

It's great here. I saw cars trucks and vans on big highways. I ate beans peas and spinach at a restaurant. I played with dogs cats and squirrels. I saw bears giraffes and lions at a zoo.

My new friends are named Pete Laura and Miguel. We play football and we also play baseball.

It's nice and warm here.

Wish you were here!

Your loving son,

Mack

Mr. and Mrs. Potter
25 Edinburgh Dr.
Fayetteville,
North Carolina
28303

Notes for Home: Your child used commas to separate items in a series. ***Home Activity:*** Make a list of foods you enjoy and have your child write sentences describing them. Have your child use commas. (For example: *I like apples, cookies, and chicken.*)

Name ______________________________

REVIEW

Commas

Directions: Add a comma or commas to correct each sentence.

1. Sonya Pam and George are in the same art class.
2. They use paints crayons and clay.
3. They had an assignment to draw paint or sculpt their houses.
4. Sonya draws with crayons colored pencils and markers.
5. George's mom lives at 16 Cactus Court Oakland CA 94601.
6. George's dad lives in Houston Texas.
7. George can draw his mom's house and Sonya can paint some flowers.
8. Pam might draw a picture or she might sculpt a model.
9. Pam loves to draw but she doesn't like crayons.
10. The assignment is due on Monday March 10.

Directions: Use a comma and conjunction to combine each pair of sentences into one compound sentence. Write the new sentence on the line.

11. I want to go to art school. My sister wants to be an astronaut.

____

12. I like to go to the art museum. She likes to go to the science museum.

____

13. We are different in many ways. We still like each other.

____

14. My sister likes my paintings. I like her models of the planets.

____

15. My sister shows me stars through a telescope. I show her how to draw them.

____

____

Notes for Home: Your child used commas in compound sentences, series, dates, and addresses. ***Home Activity:*** Ask your child to write four sentences about himself or herself. The sentences should include commas. Discuss when commas are needed.

Name ______________________________

Quotations

Quotation marks show the exact words of a speaker. Use a comma to separate the speaker's words in quotations from the rest of the sentence. Begin a quotation with a capital letter.

John said, "I have lots of homework."

In this sentence, *I* is the first word John said, and *homework* is the last. Quotation marks show the beginning (") and end (") of his speech.

Put the punctuation mark that ends the sentence inside the quotation marks. If the quotation is a question or an exclamation, put a question mark or an exclamation mark inside the quotation marks.

"Do you need any help?" his dad asked.

Directions: Punctuate each sentence correctly. Add quotation marks (" "), commas, and other punctuation marks as needed.

1. I want to go to Space Camp I said.
2. Dad said I will think about it.
3. Can we just go and take a tour I asked.
4. We can go on Saturday Mom promised.
5. I woke up and wondered Is today Saturday?
6. Yes, it is Dad exclaimed.
7. Then let's go and see Space Camp! I shouted.
8. After the tour, I said That was great
9. Do you want to go to Space Camp in June Mom asked.
10. I thought and said I can't wait!

Notes for Home: Your child wrote quotations—someone's exact words. ***Home Activity:*** Tell your child about a short conversation you had with someone today. Challenge your child to write down exactly what was said and to punctuate the quotations correctly.

Name ________________________________

Quotations

Directions: Read the following paragraph. Rewrite each sentence correctly on the lines. Check to make sure that you have put capital letters, commas, and quotation marks in the right places.

Can I interview you I asked the astronaut. Why do you want to interview me he asked. It is for the school paper I said. The astronaut said that is no problem. I asked how many times have you been in space? I have gone three times he said. What do you like best about space I asked. I love looking down at Earth he replied. Why do you love doing that I asked. The astronaut said it looks so beautiful from space.

1. ________________________________

2. ________________________________

3. ________________________________

4. ________________________________

5. ________________________________

6. ________________________________

7. ________________________________

8. ________________________________

9. ________________________________

10. ________________________________

Conduct an Interview

Interview a family member or friend you know who has done something fun or exciting. On a separate sheet of paper, write down what you both said. Use commas, quotation marks, capital letters, and other punctuation marks correctly.

Notes for Home: Your child wrote and punctuated quotations—a speaker's exact words. ***Home Activity:*** Ask your child to explain the rules for writing and punctuating quotations. Invite your child to use example sentences to help her or him explain.

Name ____________________

Quotations

RETEACHING

Quotation marks show a speaker's exact words. Rewrite the following sentence, using quotation marks.

Gina asked Why don't we go have lunch now?

____

When you write a conversation, use **quotation marks** to show the exact words of each speaker. Remember to use a comma to separate the speaker's words in quotation marks from the rest of the sentence.

Directions: Add a comma and quotation marks where they are needed.

1. Taylor said Look at these skis!
2. Philip replied They're an old pair.
3. Mr. Linn asked Would you like to see some more?
4. Yes, these skis are interesting Taylor answered.
5. Philip called There are some more over here.
6. Mr. Linn said Early skis were wooden.
7. People used skis of different lengths he added.
8. Philip asked Why did they do that?
9. Mr. Linn replied A short ski was for pushing.
10. Taylor asked Was a long ski for gliding?
11. Philip laughed That's not how people ski today!
12. Early skiers used only one pole Mr. Linn said.

Notes for Home: Your child added commas and quotation marks to signal a speaker's exact words. ***Home Activity:*** Invite your child to listen to a conversation between you and another family member. Challenge him or her to write and punctuate three quotations correctly.

Name ______________________

Quotations

Directions: Proofread each sentence. Then rewrite each one. Remember these rules about punctuating quotations:

- Use quotation marks to show the exact words of a speaker.
- Use a comma to separate the quotation from the rest of the sentence.

1. Mrs. Hackaday said here's my New Year's wish

____

2. She said i hope we all get along better this year

____

3. Sam said who doesn't get along in this class

____

4. Lucas yelled i get along with everyone

____

5. Lee said we can all try to be nicer to each other

____

6. All the students said we agree

____

Write a Dialogue

Imagine a conversation between two cartoon characters. Write what they would say to each other. Remember to use a comma and quotation marks when you write their exact words.

Notes for Home: Your child corrected quotations by adding punctuation. ***Home Activity:*** Together, write a fairy tale with your child as the main character. Challenge your child to use quotation marks correctly to show the characters are speaking.

Name ______________________________

Irregular Verbs

REVIEW

Directions: Write the correct form of each irregular verb on the line.

The Verb	The –*s* Form	The –*ing* Form	The Past Tense Form
1. swim	________	________	________
2. sing	________	________	________
3. buy	________	________	________
4. think	________	________	________

Directions: Circle the correct past-tense form of the verb in ( ) to complete each sentence.

5. Last night I (dreamded/dreamt) the strangest dream.

6. A lion almost (eated/ate) us in our own house!

7. I (saw/seed) it coming toward me.

8. I (telled/told) the lion that he was very rude.

9. He (said/sayed) he was really hungry.

10. So we (maked/made) a snack from peanut butter and bananas.

Directions: Write the correct present-tense form for each underlined past-tense verb to complete each sentence.

________________ **11.** My family <u>went</u> on a picnic.

________________ **12.** I <u>saw</u> some ants near our food.

________________ **13.** One ant <u>took</u> a cookie crumb.

________________ **14.** Two more ants <u>ran</u> by with a piece of a potato chip.

________________ **15.** I <u>began</u> to wonder if we brought enough food for everyone!

Notes for Home: Your child identified and used irregular verbs—verbs that do not add *-ed* when they are used in the past tense. ***Home Activity:*** Make a list of irregular verbs with your child. Invite your child to make up sentences using these verbs in different tenses.

Name ______________________________

Subject-Verb Agreement

The subject and verb in a sentence must work together, or **agree.** To make most present-tense verbs agree with singular subjects, add **-s.** If the subject is plural, the present-tense verb does not end in **-s.**

Singular Subject	Verb	Plural Subject	Verb
Ana	plays.	Ana and Keith	play.
He	jumps.	They	jump.
She	skips.	We	skip.
It	waddles.	You	waddle.
The duck	quacks.	The ducks	quack.

Directions: Circle the correct verb in ( ) to complete each sentence. Write the verb on the line.

______________ **1.** One ant (walk/walks) through the grass.

______________ **2.** She (meet/meets) another ant by the house.

______________ **3.** The two ants (stop/stops) to talk.

______________ **4.** It (start/starts) to rain.

______________ **5.** The ants (decide/decides) to go inside to get dry.

Directions: Write the correct form of the verb in ( ) to complete each sentence.

______________ **6.** The ants (climb) in through a hole in the screen door.

______________ **7.** One ant (ask) the other if she is hungry.

______________ **8.** The other ant (say) she could eat a crumb or too.

______________ **9.** They (go) to the kitchen to see what they can find.

______________ **10.** It's a tough choice, but the ants (pick) the raisin over the popcorn kernel.

Notes for Home: Your child chose verb forms to agree with singular or plural subjects. ***Home Activity:*** Make up cards with singular and plural animal subjects and present-tense verbs that are animal sounds. Have your child match subjects and verbs. *(The pigs grunt.)*.

Name ____________________

Subject-Verb Agreement

Directions: Choose the verb from the box that best completes each sentence. Write the verb on the line to the left.

buy buys	run runs	sit sits	take takes	wave waves

_______________ **1.** Mom and Dad _____ me to the circus.

_______________ **2.** They _____ the tickets, and we go in.

_______________ **3.** We _____ in seats near the front, so I can see everything.

_______________ **4.** The animals _____ quickly into the big top.

_______________ **5.** I _____ my hand at the animals.

_______________ **6.** A monkey _____ down in the seat next to me.

_______________ **7.** The monkey _____ my hat right off my head.

_______________ **8.** Then it _____ away with my hat!

_______________ **9.** From a swing high above the floor, the monkey _____ my hat at me.

_______________ **10.** Mom _____ me a new hat.

Write a Story

On a separate sheet of paper, write a short story about a visit to the circus or zoo. Tell what the different animals do. Be sure that in each sentence, the verb agrees with the subject.

Notes for Home: Your child chose the verb form that agrees with a singular subject (one) or a plural subject (more than one). ***Home Activity:*** Write the pronouns *I, she, he, it, we,* and *they.* Have your child tell a verb that works with each pronoun.

Name ________________________________

Subject-Verb Agreement

RETEACHING

Read each sentence pair. The subjects are underlined. Circle the present-tense verbs.

1. Kimi wears big hats.

   I wear big hats.

2. The flags flap in the wind.

   The flag flaps in the wind.

A verb in the present tense must agree with the noun or pronoun used in the subject of a sentence. Verbs used with **he, she,** or **it** end in **-s** or **-es.** Verbs used with **I, you, we,** and **they** do not end in **-s** or **-es.**

Directions: Complete the sentence with the correct form of the verb in ( ).

1. Lupe ____________ hats with feathers. (sell/sells)
2. They ____________ the hats on the table. (see/sees)
3. Anna ____________ the hat with the blue flower. (like/likes)
4. It ____________ in the dark. (glow/glows)
5. Calvin ____________ the hat with a red band. (buy/buys)
6. You ____________ a hat to Dad. (give/gives)

Directions: Write each sentence with the present-tense form of the verb in ( ).

7. Deon (wear) it proudly.

   ____

8. It (look) so fine on him.

   ____

9. We (buy) the handsome hat quickly.

   ____

Notes for Home: Your child completed sentences with verbs. ***Home Activity:*** Have your child name a subject. Say two verbs—one that goes with the subject, and one that does not—and challenge your child to choose the correct one. *(The rabbit; hop, hops.)*

Name ______________________________

Subject-Verb Agreement

Directions: Rewrite each caption that tells what students are doing to help wildlife. Make sure the subject and verb in each caption agree. Remember, to make most present-tense verbs agree with singular subjects, add **-s.**

José feed the birds.

1. ______________________________

Two friends builds a birdhouse.

2. ______________________________

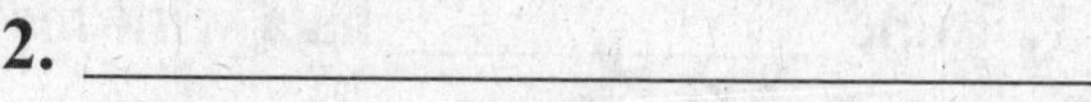

The students cleans near the stream.

3. ______________________________

____

Mira fill the bag with trash.

4. ______________________________

____

Write a Paragraph

What could you and your friends do to help the wildlife in your neighborhood? On a separate sheet of paper, write a paragraph to tell what you might do. Make sure the subjects and verbs in your sentences agree.

Notes for Home: Your child corrected captions to make subjects and verbs match. ***Home Activity:*** Look through photographs or magazine pictures and have your child write a caption about each one. Encourage him or her to make subjects and verbs match.